Iron
History and Technique

Augusto Vecchi

Iron History and Technique

© Augusto Vecchi - La Spezia (VECCHI EDITORE Srl, Italy)
© Industria Italiana Arteferro SpA -Vicenza
All rights reserved www.vecchieditore.com

Published by Artpower International Publishing Co., Ltd.

[ARTPOWER]™

Designer: Chen Ting
Chief Editor: Mo Tingli

Address: Room C, 9/F., Sun House, 181 Des Voeux Road Central, Hong Kong, China
Tel: 852-31840676
Fax: 852-25432396

Editorial Department
Address: G009, Floor 7th, Yimao Centre, Meiyuan Road, Luohu District, Shenzhen, China
Tel: 86-755-82913355
Fax: 86-755-82020029

Web: www.artpower.com.cn
E-mail: artpower@artpower.com.cn

ISBN 978-988-19973-9-5

No part of this publication may be reproduced or utilised in any form by any means, electronic or mechanical, including photocopying, recording or by any information storage and retrieval system, without prior written permission of the publisher.

All images in this book have been reproduced with the knowledge and prior consent of the designers and the clients concerned, and every effort has been made to ensure that credits accurately comply with information applied. No responsibility is accepted by producer, publisher, or printer for any infringement of copyright or otherwise arising from the contents of this publication.

Printed in China

Introduction

The term "Wrought iron" includes the concepts of hammered and notched cast iron. For many people, it becomes synonym of a kind of art which is tied to the past, or even an extinct art. In fact this viewpoint is quietly limited and even so wrong, since in recent years for many artists and artisans the productions of Blacksmith have been known as rebirth and renewed interests. As all the other materials, the iron also bears a history of ups and downs, during which the iron sometimes played a leading role and sometimes a supporting role, in comparison with all the other materials of highest value. Upon different eras when the iron was used, it has undergone a progressive evolution from the constitutive element of simple utensils to a material suitable for decoration and more precious productions. The apogee of Blacksmith creation is the baroque era, during which the architecture innovates and becomes the dance of forms and of twisted decorations. In comparison the previous eras are characterized as the most austerity.

This book refers to grill gates and gratings, which are traced back to a period from when unfortunately very few examples survived. After a short turning back to the classic and linear shapes, which are less attractive to the Blacksmith, the liberty style inaugurates a new season and makes the products of this material a big success.

This volume is dedicated to Dr. Arch. Bruno Gonzato., whose love for the Blacksmith made his company, Italian Industry Arteferro SpA, become the undisputed leader around the whole world.

Augusto Vecchi

Acknowledgement

The great parts of the present works exclusively belong to the Italian Industry Iron Art SpA. The company has granted the authorization in order to publish this book and disseminate the art of Blacksmith. Therefore, the reproduction, by any means, in any title or for any personal reason, is prohibited, even in a partial way.

Italian Industry Iron Art SpA of Mr. Gonzato was established in 1971, forging the products with dedication and constant professional enthusiasm. Being a pioneer of the Blacksmith culture, the Gonzato family has attended most of the international events of this sector, leading fashion, ideas and also the productions of perfect quality.

Now Italian Industry Iron Art SpA is not only the leader in Europe, with show rooms located in Germany, France, Spain and Scandinavia, but also around the whole world, with branches in America, Brazil, Russia and Singapore.

The workpieces presented in this book are merely a quick glance of the productions of Italian Industry Iron Art SpA. For more information, please refer to their website: www.arteferro.com.

Contents

001   *Iron Technique Overview*

007   *Grill gate*

037   *Staircase*

067   *Gratings*

233   *Furniture*

250   *Mazzucotelli*

Iron Technique Overview

One of the oldest decoration techniques, which we saw the trace in 13th century, is forging on the die or hammering. This process is applied by using one or more steel dies. The dies have different shapes and the metal plates are deformed according to the die's shape. Another technique of the decoration is etching with acid. Especially from 15th century to 18th century it is widely used to decorate the armors and other objects that require some refined processes, like casket or other precise steel instruments.

The acid is engraved into the paintings and the rest of the metal plate is covered by glass. Etching is an ancient technique of decoration and widely used in 17th and 18th century for steel objects. The painting is engraved with a steel graver which is more resistant than the decorated work piece. The depth of incision is limited by the strength of the material, but it is specially used for some delicate workpeices of doors and windows and some very specialized blacksmiths products.

The process of tempering is applied with burning heat after a sudden cooling. This application can protect the material from rust and also produce some colorful decorative effects on the locks, caskets or weapons.

Another technique, which is used especially for the silver and copper workpieces and sometimes also for the iron products, is repoussage. With it, the thin metal laminates, like iron piece, can be covered with a less resistant material and moulded with die until it obtains an ideal shape. And niello technique: an engraved design is filled with a mixture of copper, silver and sulfur; after being heated up, the inlay becomes black and contrast from the bright and clear base.

The niello technique is also called as " technique of Tula", homonymic Russian city, which was renowned center in 17th and 18th century.

Now let's discuss together the general characteristic of the iron, both the availability and problems during the production. The homogeneous iron has a feature of avoiding being more fragile and harder. This characteristic also enables the iron to easily be processed with hammer after being heated and then cooled down immediately.

Iron Technique Overview

If the iron contains some phosphorus, sulfur, arsenic, copper or any other impurities, it will become fragile and even broken when being heat processed. Instead if it contains some phosphorus, the iron can be processed on the heat, but it will become fragile when being worked on a cold end and will be broken very easily. The presence of calcium or other impurities will take away from the malleable iron the feature of being able to be welded directly. That's why the welding of iron, and generally speaking the blacksmith art, has realized a significant progresses in the entire steel industry and also in the regions which owns a lot of nice minerals.

As we implied before, the so-called "native" iron has the only minim quantity in nature. Usually it combines with nickel and other elements. It's quite common that in the mixture, we cannot distinguish which is body and which is container.

The pure iron is very malleable. It has a density of $7.86 g/m^3$, melting point is 1529 ° and boiling point is 2450°. With carbon and silicon, the iron will magnetize easily and even faster. So it's widely used for the induction devices. It has three allotropes that transform from each other according to the temperature changes.

The iron is the metal which has the most technical appliances, thanks to the facts that the features can vary greatly with even just a little more other elements or through some thermal treatment. The possible variations should happen to tenacity, hardness, elasticity, dilatability resistance to the chemicals, magnetic properties and etc.

The pure iron is never used for a technical purpose, but the iron is usually used combing with carbon, magnet, vanadium, tungsten, molybdenum, etc. The tensile strength of the iron floats from 314 to 412 N/mm^2. A precious characteristic is iron's forgeability; the malleability is connected with ferrite crystal: smaller they are, more malleable the iron is. Soft iron is a product of iron and steel with small amount of carbon and even some scoria. Soft iron is susceptible to weld itself.

In ancient times in order to prepare the soft iron, people used Catalan system, which processes directly the mineral in a bloomer (Catalan forge) with charcoal. The carbonic oxide is formed and together with glowing charcoal, it reduces the mineral in a metallic iron; it releases small pulpy masses, which are extracted from bloomer and are welded together into a large mass. The large mass is then hammered to get rid of the scoria. In this way the iron will be very pure, but the process is very long and expensive. Around 17th century, the iron starts to be processed directly into cast iron, which should eliminate extraneous elements through oxidation at high temperature. For the purpose of following different methods, for example "Bergamo" forge, in a bloomer similar as Catalan forge, the charcoal gets burning and when it is in full combustion, the cast iron is added piece by piece and mixed into bladesmithing (containing iron oxide).

In this way people burns also silicon, manganese, and carbon, when iron oxide detains sulfur and phosphor. In this way the iron is separated, quite pure in small masses which can be mixed again into a large mass with hammering.

Iron Technique Overview

In the process of "puddling", instead people use coke and reverberatory whose base is coated with iron ore (iron oxide). The reverberatory is maintained at a temperature between the melting point of cast iron (around 1100°) and that of iron (around 1500°). The oxygen of iron oxide of the base and that of the air make carbon and sulfur burn and also oxidize silicon and manganese. Gradually the cast iron is losing the carbon, its melting point is going up and the products are made in mass.

This operation is applied by keeping the mass in constant agitation by means of iron rods through the appropriate hole of the furnace from the workers. Also here the iron, which is gradually formed, is releasing the doughy lumps that can be collected and gathered into a larger mass by hammering.

With the invention of rotary kiln, people eliminate the inconvenient stirring of the masses by hand. This kiln is made from a center where the carbon burns in a cylindrical furnace called "stove" or "egg", which is revolving above rolls and holds in the rotary movement on the horizontal axis by means of a toothed wheel. The furnace of cast iron is coated inside with refractory material; the liquid iron is applied when the oxidizing flame is passing from the attached furnace; the cast iron is gradually losing its carbon and is transformed into iron mass which can be extracted and hammered.

Recently people attempt to re-acquire iron directly from the ore, but instead of using the charcoal as in the Catalan method, they use the fuel (hydrogen and carbon monoxide produced from coke).

This process is cheaper than old Catalan, and make more pure products.

Very pure iron is then obtained by electrolytic solutions of sulphate or ferrous chloride. The anodes are given by plates of iron or steel and the cathodes have different forms depending on the products you want to achieve.

The fracture surface of a good iron must be clear grey and in a fibrous structure. The tests for tension, compression and elongation are very important for the evaluation of quality; a good iron must be able to bend many times without breaking.

The test should be done on an iron block with a V-groove: take a test material with 20cm length and about 0.8cm diameter. It is beaten by a hammer in order to have a shape of V; it is straightened and bended again, but in an opposite direction as before and then straightened still. The piece must remain intact. The test should be made through heat or cool.

Other tests are made in 1200—1300°C: the rod is bended itself repeatedly; it is cracked apart and two flaps part away. If the iron is

Iron Technique Overview

Iron Technique Overview

good, it shouldn't be broken up. Or on a sheet of iron in test, some holes are punched near the end of the blade. It should neither be parted nor be split after being folded over itself on the point where it was perforated.

Finally the bar whose diameter is half of the length, placed upright on an anvil, must be able to be beaten until shrunk by one-third of its length without any cleavage.

Now let's see some practical rules for operations related to the manufacture and the maintenance of iron.

The first are real recipes, which were still adopted in the first decade of our century by each blacksmiths products, regarding burnishing, nickel, silver and gold of iron.

Today these rules begin to become rare and mystery formulas as those of necromancers. But many veteran artisans still adopted them.

A good solution to platinize the iron is as following: 3 liters water, nitric acid 60g, copper sulfate 100g, nitric acid 140g, iron tincture 15g, corrosive sublimate 135g, alcohol 130g.

The objects are coated with this solution by sponge. And they are left to dry for 30 hours and then a stiff brush is used. Then brush again second coat of the same material. And wash away with boiling water and make them dry immediately. The burnished objects are preserved with a light coat of linseed oil or varnish.

To nickel iron through immersion, in case of small objects which are difficult to deal with the electrolytic system, the procedures are the followings: the nickel sulfate is dissolved in a solution of 12% zinc chloride and it is heated until getting boiled and put in an earthen vessel. The objects to be nickeled are immersed for an hour and then get dried by plaster powder and brushed for polishing.

To prepare a powder capable of nickeling the iron and any other metal with simple scrubbing:

Mix nickel powder 30g, sulphate of ammonia 40g, magnesium 4g.

Clean and rub the objects with little powder distributed on a wet cloth.

For silver plating: rub the object with a piece of flannel which is soaked in the following mixture: distilled water 20g, hydrochloric acid of ammonia 15g, sodium chloride 55g, potassium 40g, silver chloride 30g.

For the gilding of iron and steel: to dissolve gold chloride 2g and potassium ferrocyanide 20g into 200g water. Prepare separately maximum saturated solution of potassium; by mixing together, two solutions become the liquid of gold plating which must be diluted with little water.

The pieces to be gilded are immersed in this solution: the greater or minor intensity of the gilding depends on the time of immersion; the objects extracted from the solution should be rinsed in acidulated water with sulfuric acid and rubbed with a cloth.

Iron Technique Overview

To remove the rusts, there are three diverse techniques, according to the conditions of objects. The preservation of pieces which are seriously corroded and completely covered with rusts (generally archaeological objects) is always delegated to some specialists, who mostly apply a procedure called "stabilization".

If the objects are just partially rusted or covered with unsightly traces of paint, people will use chemical method: the workpiece is cleaned with ethyl trichloride or with another degreasing, and then left for some necessary time in a solution of phosphoric acid in which inhibitor is added. The rust is then removed mechanically with a light wire brush which is used under running water. This process need be repeated, changing the solution and cleaning tools until the last trace of rust or paint disappears. The clean workpiece then is immersed in a solution of 3%-5% phosphorus and finally dried well with a cloth and then with hot air.

To ensure the objects will not be attached by rust in short, it is still immersed in a solution of silicon or covered with a transparent varnish or one of special types of wax products.

And please pay attention that the methods do not give a shiny surface to the iron, which is contrary to the natural quality of the metal. The pieces which are too large to be immersed in the solution, should be cleaned with a paste which contains phosphoric acid.

In the case of tempered iron (for example the springs for locks) or iron combined with other metals, the process described above for removing the rust is contra-indicated. A technique called "tannin" should be adopted: the objects should be degreased and then cleaned with a horsehair brush or metal impregnated with a solution of tannin, distilled water and alcohol, which removes the rust, leaving a black surface for oxidation. If a smooth or polished iron surface has only patches of rusts, they can be removed by refined petrol or methylcyclohexanol. The object should be polished with a felt cloth or flannel and degreased and treated in the usual way for storage. The collector can keep the iron in an environment of normal temperature, and it is especially important that the relative humidity of the environment shouldn't fall below 55%.

Grill gates

Production: Italian Industry Iron Art SpA

Grill gate

Grill gate of the 1980s' style

Grill gate

Grill gate at the entrance of Baracchini Villa, in Sarzana, La Spezia, Italy.

Grill gate

Above and following are details of grill gate of Barachini Villa

Grill gate

From the beginning the grill gate is entirely made from woods and functions precisely by allowing the transit from a fence which defines the space. But later the gate starts to be made also with some metallic parts, as an addition to the wood parts, in order to make the structure more solid and enduring. Moreover, as iron being a very resistant material, it can provide the gate the function of safety protection.

The portion of the iron is then going up and finally it becomes the unique material, with which various gates are built both inside and outside the buildings.

That is the historical moment, when the iron becomes not only a defensive element but also a sort of "mobile wall" that both connect and divide the space between public and private at the same time.

Grill gate

Grill gate

According to the stylistic and architectural criteria of different eras, the grill gate experiences a significant change from the simple and linear shapes of the Middle Age to a fully decorated style of the 16th and the 17th century. The grill gates which are made from the 18th century to Renaissance period, show many similar characters, because the ornamental theme of cornices or frame of the grill gates mainly lies in unifying vegetal motifs with zoomorphic subjects; or reusing the shape of harpoons or bunch of stylish flowers.

Grill gate

Moreover the typical grill gate of 15th century presents a structure formed by cross-posts with horizontal bars, which together give rise to many compartments containing quatredoil motif, which are always replicated from each other for all the work. The coping is certainly the element that mostly distinguishes the gates at different times and it is the one that undertakes the most changes of shapes.

In fact the decoration of grill gates becomes more and more complex until being represented by dense texture of leaves, flowers and tendrils.

The abundance of decorations increases with the passage of time and reaches its peak in the Baroque Age. While in earlier times the decorations with plant motifs were organized in horizontal bands that stood at the top of the gates, instead in the Baroque times, foliage and floral motifs pervade aggressively every part of the workpieces, from the bars of the gates to the fanlight of the doors.

17th Century

Grill gate near church S. Francesco in Ferrara

17th Century

Grill gate near church S. Marco in Roma

Grill gate

French grill gate of blacksmith ornamentalist Michelin

Grill gate

French grill gate of blacksmith ornamentalist Michelin

Grill gate

Grill gate of Siena, 18th century production

In addition, the blacksmiths products are enriched in this period with new elements.

The columns of the grill gates are no longer limited in horizontal bars, but are delimitated by friezes and high wainscoting on the lower part. The coping, made in the shape of real large branches of flowers or the miniature of trees on which the snakes that swallow the human beings are all twisted, faded gradually.

Grill gate

Grill gate of French-style modern production

Grill gate

Grill gate of modern production- Micheluzzi, Pistoia.

Grill gate

Grill gate at the entrance of Groppallo Villa, Sarzana SP.

Grill gate

Specifics of the grill gate

The main characters of Baroque architectures lie in the fancifulness and dynamism of the shapes. These attributes are used as elements by the buildings and decorations of urban center, which become parts of a unique and magnificent design.

With extreme use of its malleable nature, the iron is used in a particular way for this type of products which constantly contribute to the redundancy of the shapes and the complexity of the lines.

Grill gate

Grill gate

Grill gate

However, as other architectural elements, the grill gate achieved a new stage in Baroque Age. A series of gates are respectively present along different long lanes which stretch to the memorial square.

The most famous grill gates of this relative concept are located in the palaces, state courts and parks. They look like an ideal curtain, as those in Palace of Versaille, Schloss Belvedere in Vienna and The Palazzina di caccia of Stupinigi in Turin.

Dating back to Baroque Age the Italian grill gates use more simple lines than gates of other countries. The masterpiece of this period should be the grill gate of Real Villa of Milan, which copies the imperial emblems of Napoleon, and the grill gate at the entrance of Annalena in the Boboli garden in Firenze, which shows all the essential characters of Baroque Age.

Grill gate

Grill gate at the entrance of Malaspina Villa, in Sarzana, SP

Grill gate

Secondary entrance of Malaspina Villa, in Sarzana, SP

Grill gate

We should define the Baroque Age as a period when all the blacksmith products experience the biggest boost, both in the area of artistic research, where more and more twisted simple lines and composition of multiple ornaments are used, and also in the area of great urban restoration between the 17th and the 18th centuries, which lead to the destruction of entire city centers and their complete restructuring according to the architectural canons of the era.

Of course the blacksmith doesn't prevail in all the ages as the best expression of art and functions. In fact immediately after the Baroque Age, it is replaced by a new tendency, which requires returning to the simplicity of shapes and the purity of style. It is identified as classism. During the neo-classism, the manufacture of iron is limited to the creation of simple shapes and especially to decorative objects, which have certain functions but are short of decorations or to the ornaments which can only suffocate the pure shape.

Grill gate

Another secondary entrance of Malaspina Villa

Grill gate

Products : Ind.i.a SPA

The transfer to a conception so diametrically contrary to that of Baroque Age is one of the causes of the minor production of the grill gates of blacksmith, due to both decoration and defense concerns.

In the period of neo-classism, the traditional themes of the grill gates have gone back to the arrows and other defensive elements with practical functions, as to obstruct the furtive transit above the grill gate and block the pigeons and other birds.

Grill gate

Products: Ind.i.a SPA

The artists, who make the blacksmiths products in the 19th century, mostly take inspiration from the old products and the traditional theme of 16th century. Sometimes they even entirely copy the blacksmith predecessor's production. The blacksmith products experience a period of revival with the liberty style, which brings back the study of decorations, embellishment and curve and sinuous lines of Baroque Age. The characteristic of liberty grill gates is a kind of very delicate decoration of floral mortifs which pervades the whole era.

Grill gate

Products : Ind.i.a SPA

Grill gate

French grill gate of modern production

Grill gate

Entrance of Villa Piovene, Lugo, Vicenza

Grill gate

Products : Ind.i.a SPA

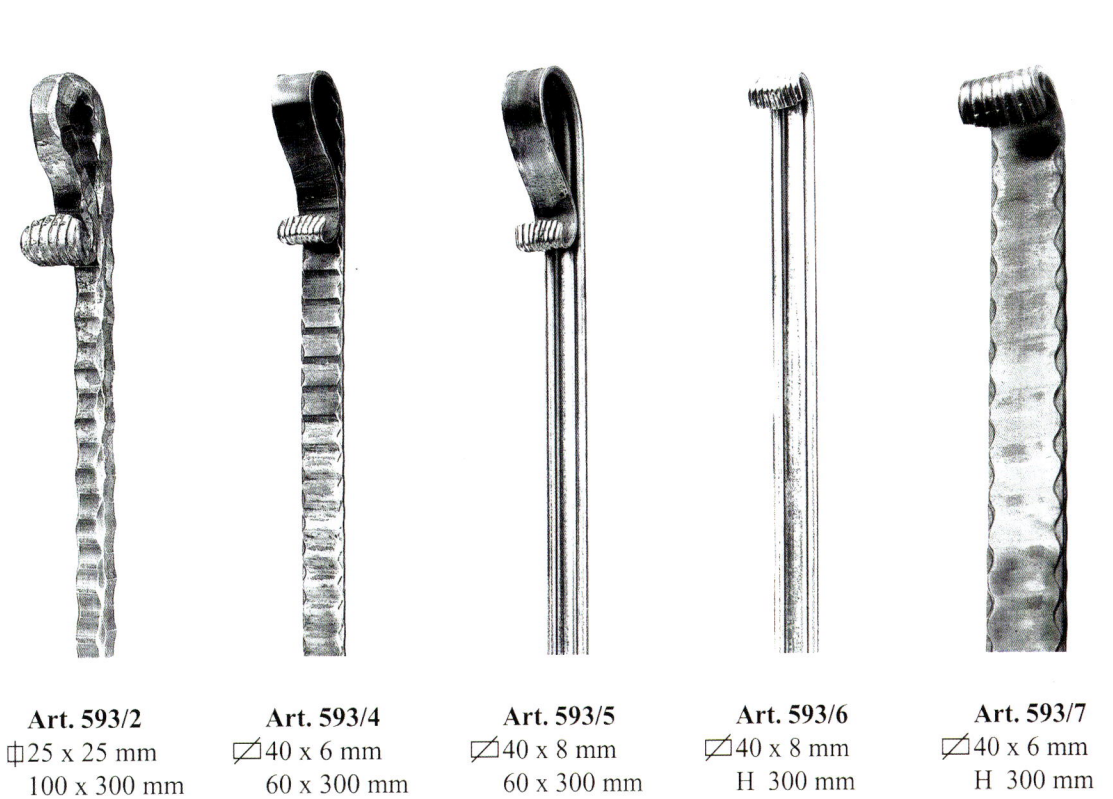

Grill gate

Art. 593/9
⏹ 14 x 14 mm
H 900 mm

Art. 593/8
⏹ 14 x 14 mm
H 900 mm

Art. 593/2	Art. 593/4	Art. 593/5	Art. 593/6	Art. 593/7
⏹ 25 x 25 mm	⬙ 40 x 6 mm	⬙ 40 x 8 mm	⬙ 40 x 8 mm	⬙ 40 x 6 mm
100 x 300 mm	60 x 300 mm	60 x 300 mm	H 300 mm	H 300 mm

035

Grill gate

Art. 509/1
H 900 mm ca.

Products : Ind.i.a SPA

Staircase

Products : Ind.i.aSPA

Staircase

Art. 94/E/1
460 x 440 x 12 mm

Art. 112/6
⌀ 30 mm
H 1200 mm

Art. 2011/9
⌀ 70 mm

Art. 94/C/1
130 x 100 x 4 mm

Art. 94/A/6
80 x 80 x 8 mm

Art. 94/C/2
170 x 140 x 4 mm

Art. 115/1

Produzione: ind.i.a. SPA

Staircase

With the staircase parts, we would understand the enormous success of blacksmith products in the area of architecture and furniture. It is iron's peculiarity of lightness and high resistance that make all the iron staircases obtain an amazing lightness and a very high decorative value, both for the railing and other supporting iron parts of stairs. The blacksmith artworks can be traced back to Europe in the beginning of the Millennium. The ornamental pieces are processed by welding, punching, hammering and twisting.

Staircase

Art. 24/E/1
⏂ 12 x 12 mm
⌀ 600 mm

Art. 114/2
58 x 14 mm
L 2000 mm

Art. 2016/8
⏂ 12 x 12 mm
⌀ 100 mm

Art. 113/10
⌀ 70 mm

Art. 24/F/2
⏂ 12 x 12 mm
300 x 220 mm

Art. 115/2

Produzione: ind.i.a. SPA

040

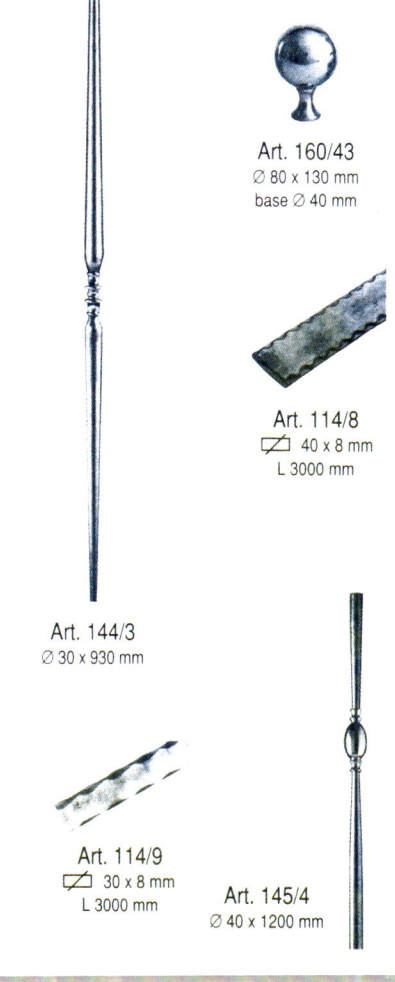

Staircase

Art. 160/43
⌀ 80 x 130 mm
base ⌀ 40 mm

Art. 114/8
40 x 8 mm
L 3000 mm

Art. 144/3
⌀ 30 x 930 mm

Art. 114/9
30 x 8 mm
L 3000 mm

Art. 145/4
⌀ 40 x 1200 mm

Produzione: ind.i.a. SPA

041

Staircase

Art. 119/25
⟐ 20 x 20 mm
H 1000 mm

Art. 111/3
⟐ 30 x 30 mm
H 1200 mm
⌀ 70 mm

Art. 116/B/2
58 x 14 mm

Art. 114/9
30 x 8 mm
L 3000 mm

Art. 116/B1
58 x 14 mm
L 2000 mm

Art. 94/A/6
80 x 80 x 8 mm

Produzione: ind.i.a. SPA

042

Staircase

Staircase

Art. 105/2
H 900 mm ca.

Art. 105/1
H 900 mm ca.

Art. 112/7
⌀ 25 mm
H 1200 mm

Art. 114/B/13

Art. 116/A/2
5 mm
75 x 75 mm

Art. 116/A/17
⌀ 72 mm

Art. 114/A/3
47 x 16 mm
L 3000 mm

Art. 2018/5
245 x 900 mm

Art. 114/9
30 x 8 mm
L 3000 mm

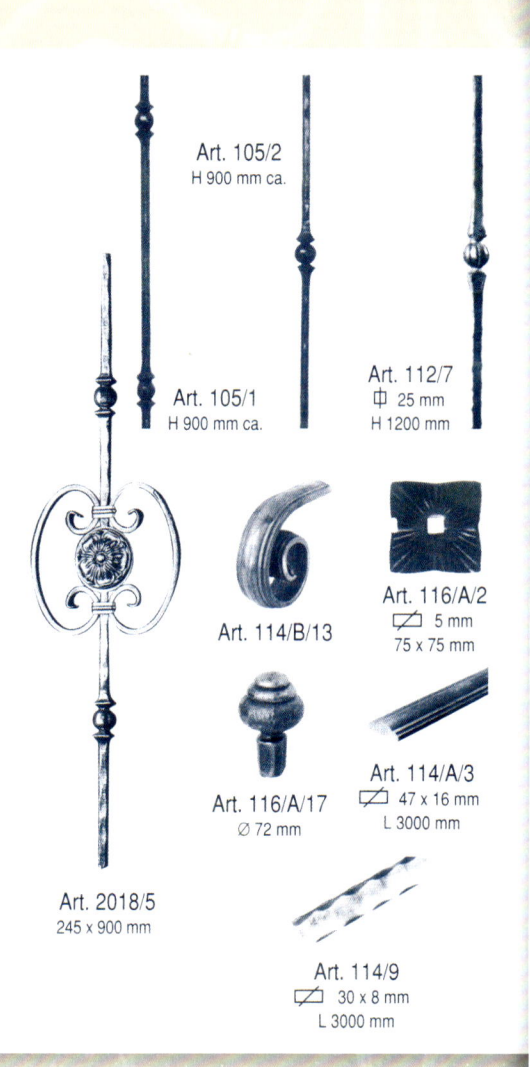

Produzione: ind.i.a. SPA

Staircase

Art. 113/10
⌀ 70 mm

Art. 94/B/5
105 x 4 mm

Art. 94/C/1
130 x 100 x 4 mm

Art. 94/F/1
Art. 94/F/2
690 x 320 x 12 mm

Art. 94/C/3
Art. 94/C/4
170 x 110 x 10 mm

Art. 94/F/3
Art. 94/F/4
800 x 490 x 12 mm

Art. 94/F/5
Art. 94/F/6
970 x 420 x 12 mm

Art. 94/B/3
220 x 115 x 4 mm

Produzione: ind.i.a. SPA

Staircase

Art. 105/2
H 900 mm ca.

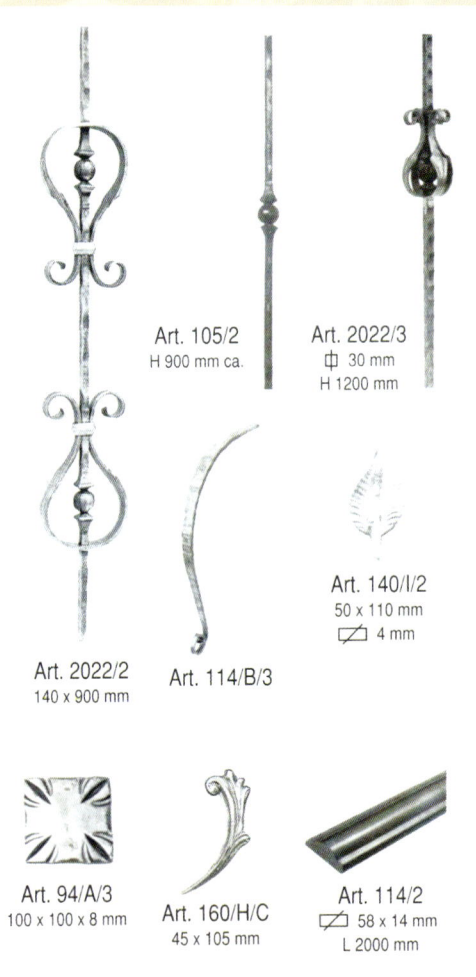

Art. 2022/3
⌯ 30 mm
H 1200 mm

Art. 2022/2
140 x 900 mm

Art. 114/B/3

Art. 140/I/2
50 x 110 mm
4 mm

Art. 94/A/3
100 x 100 x 8 mm

Art. 160/H/C
45 x 105 mm

Art. 114/2
58 x 14 mm
L 2000 mm

Produzione: ind.i.a. SPA

Staircase

Art. 112/6
☐ 30 mm
H 1200 mm

Art. 52/1
◇ 12 x 6 mm
350 x 870 mm

Art. 115/2

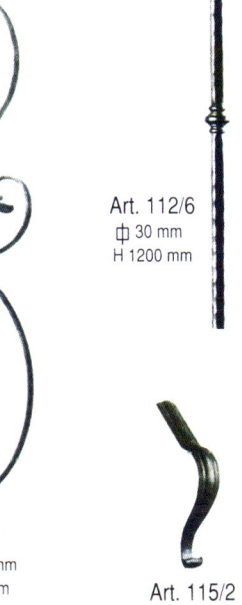

Art. 116/A/20
⌀ 55 mm

Art. 114/2
◇ 58 x 14 mm
L 2000 mm

Art. 114/3
◇ 30 x 10 mm
L 3000 mm

Produzione: ind.i.a. SPA

Staircase

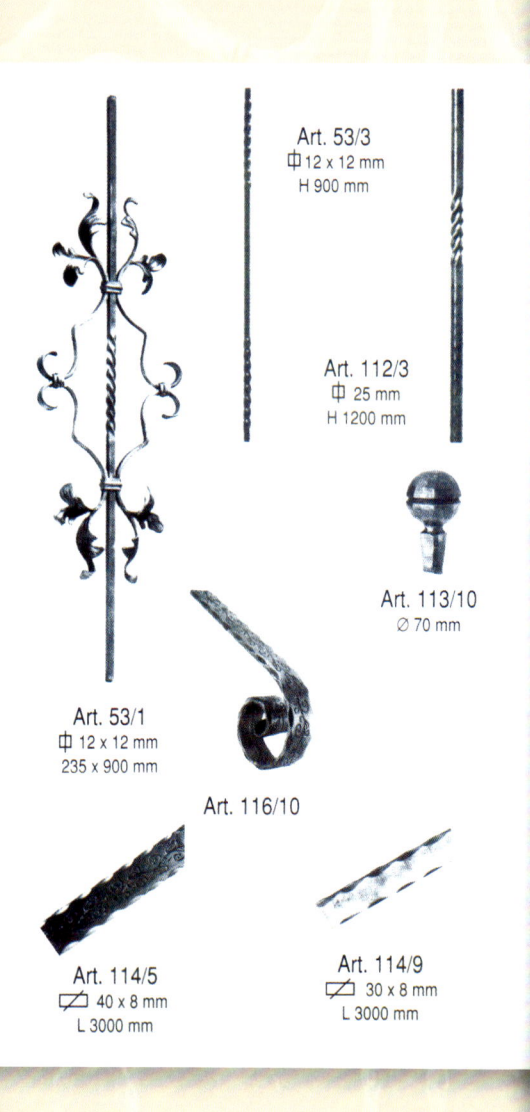

Art. 53/3
⌑ 12 x 12 mm
H 900 mm

Art. 112/3
⌀ 25 mm
H 1200 mm

Art. 113/10
⌀ 70 mm

Art. 53/1
⌑ 12 x 12 mm
235 x 900 mm

Art. 116/10

Art. 114/5
◇ 40 x 8 mm
L 3000 mm

Art. 114/9
◇ 30 x 8 mm
L 3000 mm

Produzione: ind.i.a. SPA

048

Staircase

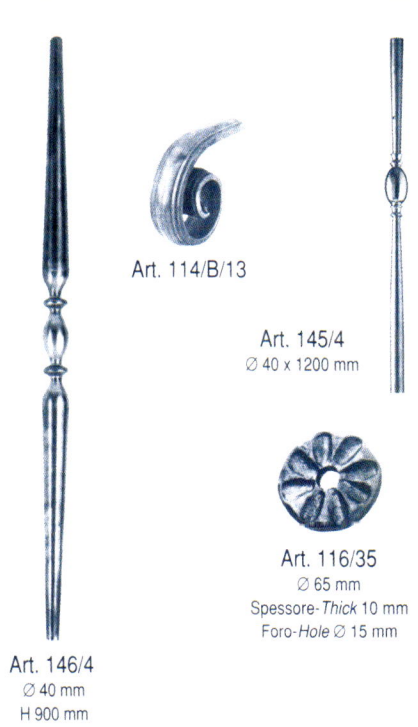

Art. 114/B/13

Art. 145/4
⌀ 40 x 1200 mm

Art. 116/35
⌀ 65 mm
Spessore-*Thick* 10 mm
Foro-*Hole* ⌀ 15 mm

Art. 146/4
⌀ 40 mm
H 900 mm

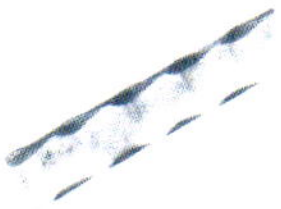

Art. 114/9
30 x 8 mm
L 3000 mm

Art. 114/A/3
47 x 16 mm
L 3000 mm

Produzione: ind.i.a. SPA

Staircase

Art. 112/8
□ 30 mm
H 1200 mm

Art. 148/2
⌀ 30 mm
H 900 mm

Art. 116/2

Art. 114/5
◇ 40 x 8 mm
L 3000 mm

Art. 113/9
⌀ 75 mm

Produzione: ind.i.a. SPA

050

Staircase

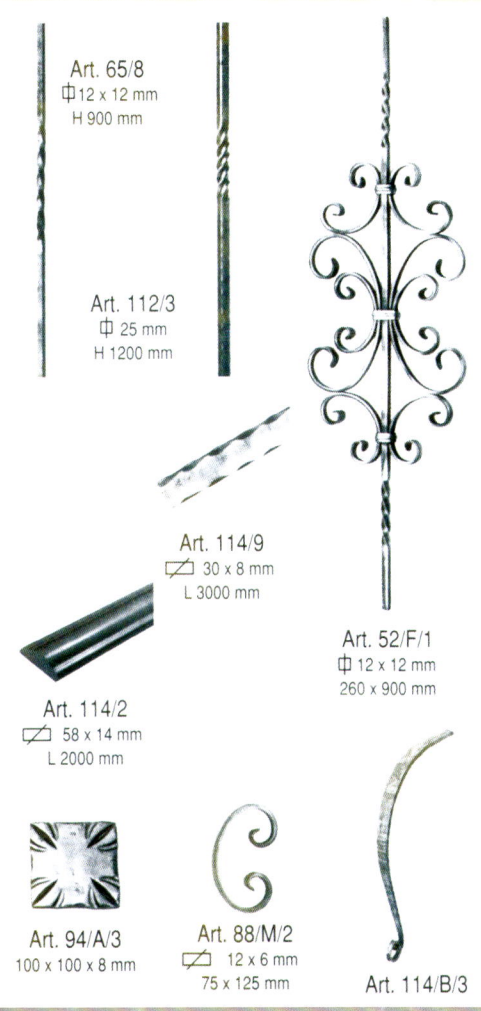

Art. 65/8
⌷ 12 x 12 mm
H 900 mm

Art. 112/3
⌀ 25 mm
H 1200 mm

Art. 114/9
◊ 30 x 8 mm
L 3000 mm

Art. 52/F/1
⌷ 12 x 12 mm
260 x 900 mm

Art. 114/2
◊ 58 x 14 mm
L 2000 mm

Art. 94/A/3
100 x 100 x 8 mm

Art. 88/M/2
◊ 12 x 6 mm
75 x 125 mm

Art. 114/B/3

Produzione: ind.i.a. SPA

051

Staircase

Staircase

Art. 116/2

Art. 113/10
Ø 70 mm

Art. 134/B/4
☐ 12 x 12 mm
H 900 mm

Art. 134/B/6
☐ 12 x 12 mm
H 900 mm

Art. 114/5
◇ 40 x 8 mm
L 3000 mm

Art. 114/9
◇ 30 x 8 mm
L 3000 mm

Produzione: ind.i.a. SPA

Staircase

Art. 112/9
⌀ 30 mm
H 1200 mm

Art. 142/B/1
H 820 mm

Art. 116/2

Art. 114/5
40 x 8 mm
L 3000 mm

Art. 114/9
30 x 8 mm
L 3000 mm

Produzione: ind.i.a. SPA

Staircase

Art. 114/2
58 x 14 mm
L 2000 mm

Art. 114/9
30 x 8 mm
L 3000 mm

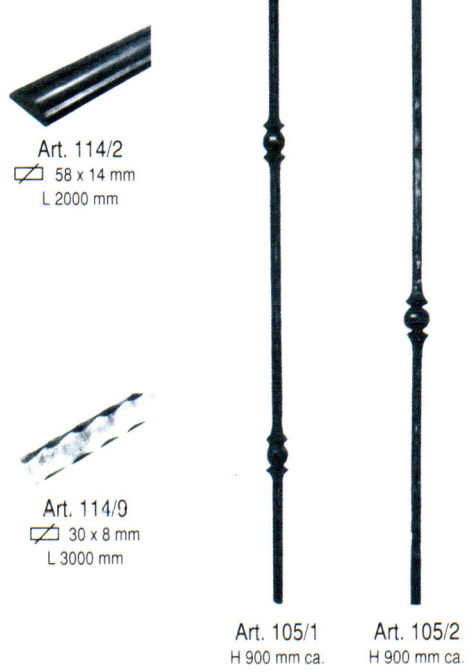

Art. 105/1
H 900 mm ca.

Art. 105/2
H 900 mm ca.

Art. 115/3

Art. 113/9
⌀ 75 mm

Produzione: ind.i.a. SPA

Staircase

Art. 116/A/2
◇ 5 mm
75 x 75 mm

Art. 113/7
⊡ 20 x 20 mm
1100 mm

Art. 2007/1
⊡ 8 x 8 mm
145 x 900 mm

79

Produzione: ind.i.a. SPA

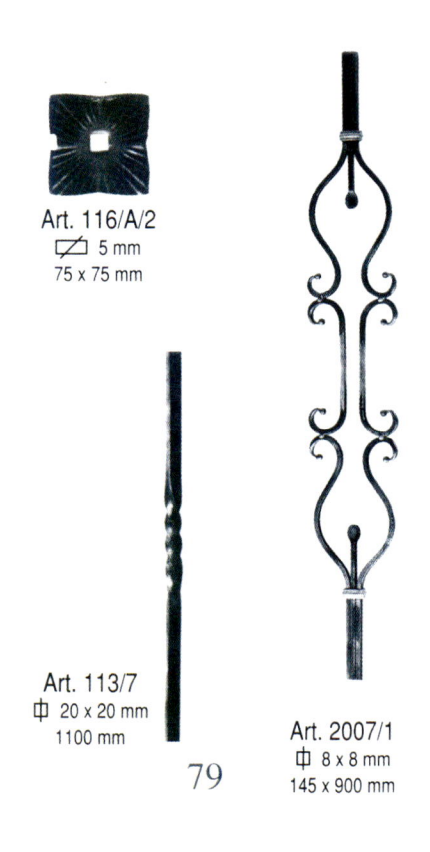

056

Staircase

Staircase

Art. 116/2

Art. 113/10
Ø 70 mm

Art. 70/E/2
◻ 12 x 12 mm
H 820 mm

Art. 114/9
30 x 8 mm
L 3000 mm

Art. 114/5
40 x 8 mm
L 3000 mm

Produzione: ind.i.a. SPA

058

Staircase

Art. 64/F/4
⏹ 12 x 12 mm
H 900 mm

Art. 64/F/1
⏹ 25 x 25 mm
H 1200 mm

Art. 116/A/17
⌀ 72 mm

Art. 64/G/1
⏹ 12 x 12 mm
225 x 900 mm

Art. 116/2

Art. 114/9
30 x 8 mm
L 3000 mm

Art. 114/5
40 x 8 mm
L 3000 mm

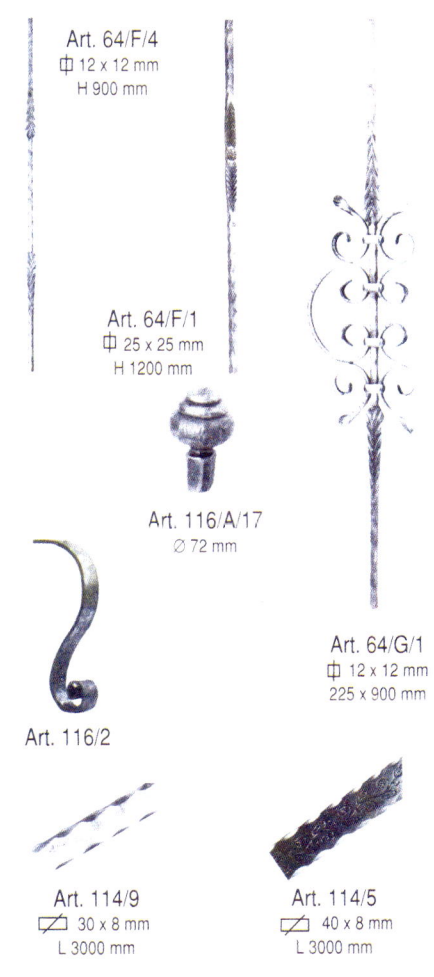

Produzione: ind.i.a. SPA

059

Staircase

Art. 64/F/3
□ 14 x 14 mm
H 900 mm

Art. 113/1
□ 20 x 20 mm
H 1100 mm

Art. 113/9
Ø 75 mm

Art. 2008/11
□ 14 x 14 mm
900 mm

Art. 116/2

Produzione: ind.i.a. SPA

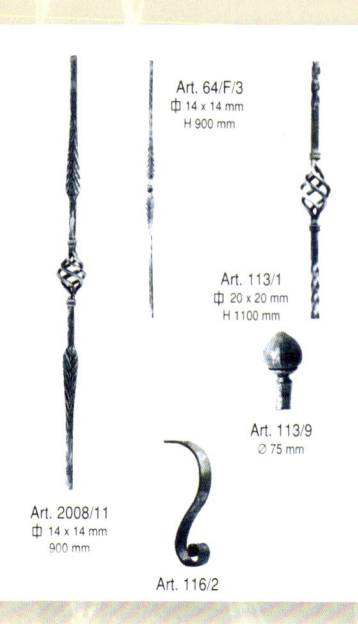

Art. 160/D/12
Ø 40 x 135 mm
foro-hole Ø 16 mm

Art. 118/A/29
Ø 16 mm
L 3000 mm

Art. 118/A/31
Ø 20 mm
L 3000 mm

Art. 116/A/2
□ 5 mm
75 x 75 mm

Art. 116/A/7
□ 10 mm
100 x 100 mm

Art. 116/A/18
Ø 60 mm

Art. 160/D/13
Ø 40 x 135 mm
foro-hole Ø 20 mm

Art. 114/B/13

060

Staircase

Art. 118/H/1
Φ 12 x 12 mm
H 900 mm

Art. 113/1
Φ 20 x 20 mm
H 1100 mm

Art. 116/10

Art. 2004/1
Φ 12 x 12 mm
230 x 900 mm

Art. 114/9
30 x 8 mm
L 3000 mm

Art. 114/5
40 x 8 mm
L 3000 mm

Produzione: ind.i.a. SPA

061

Staircase

Art. 116/2

Art. 113/10
Ø 70 mm

Art. 134/A/7
12 x 6 mm
H 900 mm

Art. 134/A/9
12 x 6 mm
H 900 mm

Art. 114/5
40 x 8 mm
L 3000 mm

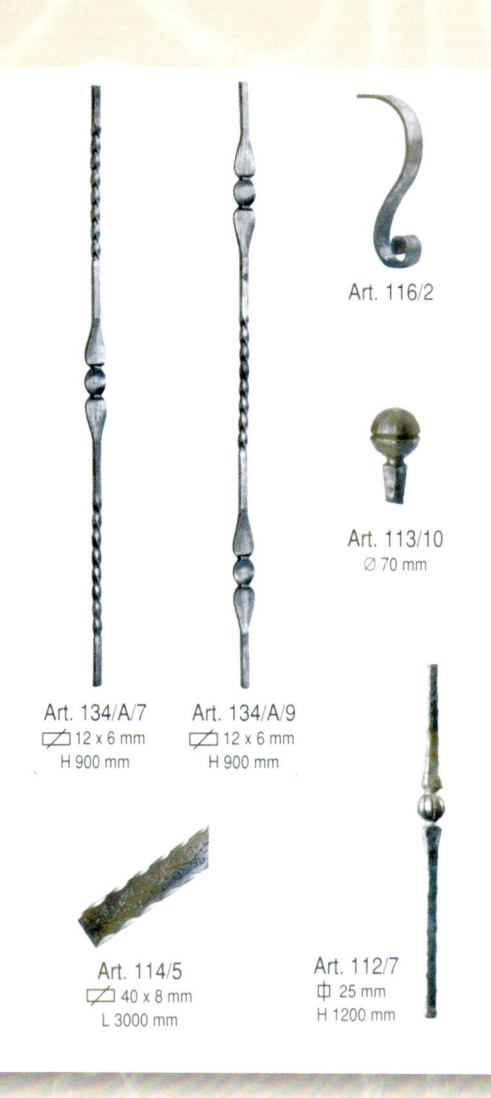

Art. 112/7
25 mm
H 1200 mm

Produzione: ind.i.a. SPA

Staircase

Art. 53/3
⌑ 12 x 12 mm
H 900 mm

Art. 116/10

Art. 64/A/1
⌑ 12 x 12 mm
250 x 900 mm

Art. 113/10
⌀ 70 mm

Art. 114/5
▱ 40 x 8 mm
L 3000 mm

Art. 114/9
▱ 30 x 8 mm
L 3000 mm

Produzione: ind.i.a. SPA

063

Staircase

Art. 64/F/3
⬜ 14 x 14 mm
H 900 mm

Art. 112/7
⬜ 25 mm
H 1200 mm

Art. 2018/3
⬜ 14 x 14 mm
100 x 900 mm

Art. 115/3

Art. 113/12
⌀ 80 mm

Art. 116/A/1
▱ 5 mm
70 x 70 mm

Art. 114/3
▱ 30 x 10 mm
L 3000 mm

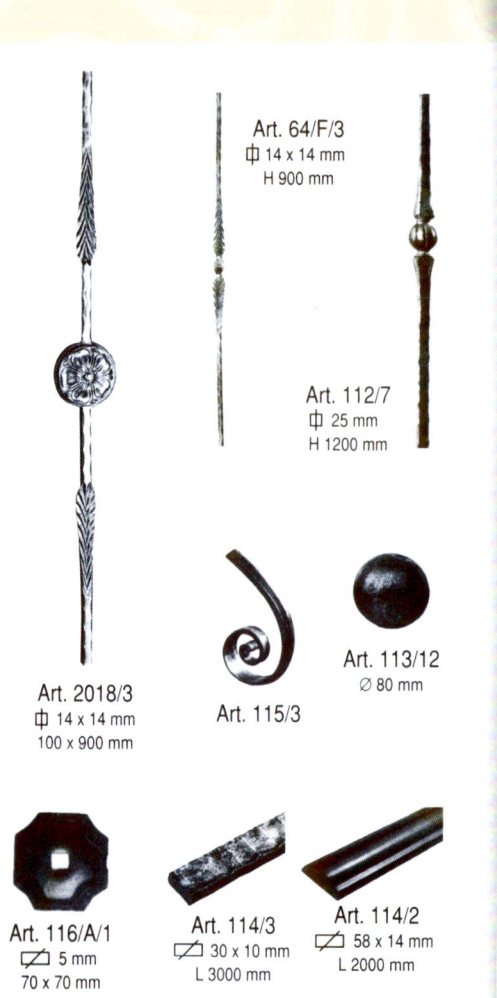

Art. 114/2
▱ 58 x 14 mm
L 2000 mm

Produzione: ind.i.a. SPA

064

Staircase

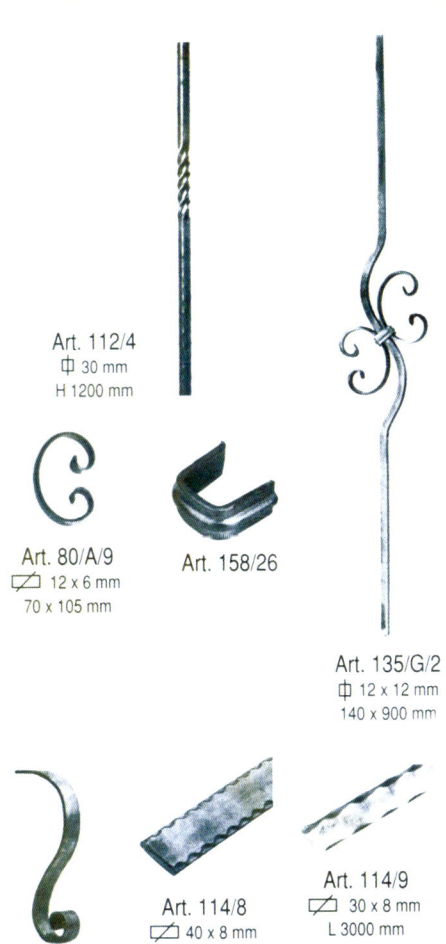

Art. 112/4
⬜ 30 mm
H 1200 mm

Art. 80/A/9
▱ 12 x 6 mm
70 x 105 mm

Art. 158/26

Art. 135/G/2
⬜ 12 x 12 mm
140 x 900 mm

Art. 116/5

Art. 114/8
▱ 40 x 8 mm
L 3000 mm

Art. 114/9
▱ 30 x 8 mm
L 3000 mm

Produzione: ind.i.a. SPA

Staircase

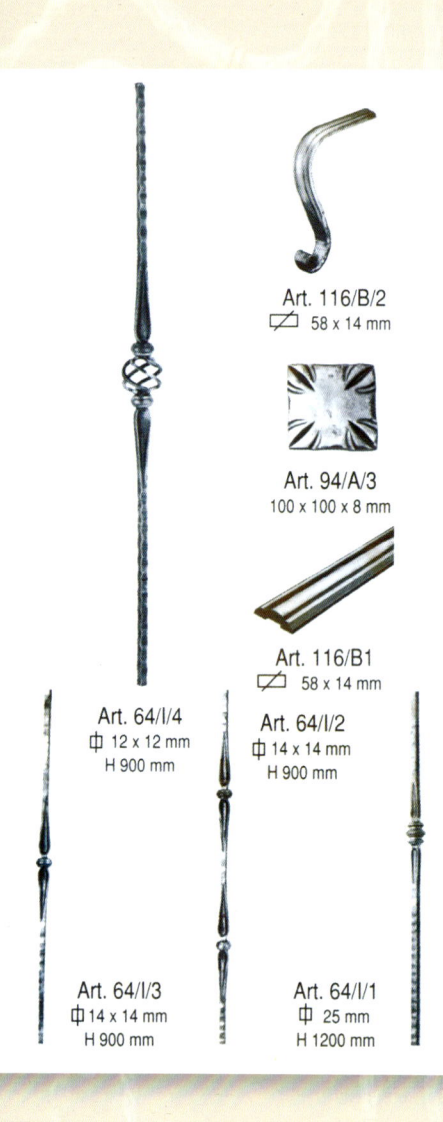

Art. 116/B/2
58 x 14 mm

Art. 94/A/3
100 x 100 x 8 mm

Art. 116/B1
58 x 14 mm

Art. 64/I/4
12 x 12 mm
H 900 mm

Art. 64/I/2
14 x 14 mm
H 900 mm

Art. 64/I/3
14 x 14 mm
H 900 mm

Art. 64/I/1
25 mm
H 1200 mm

Produzione: ind.i.a. SPA

066

Gratings

Products: Ind.i.a SPA

Gratings

Gratings

The grating includes: parapets of balcony, grills of windows, roofs or railings of the staircase. You can see that all of them are essential elements for either a public or a private building. The grating especially determines the elegance of the building.

As for the grill gate, people can distinguish the gratings from different phases of developments and various styles in different times. In fact generally in order to make the entire building have a harmony style, the grating shares the same development as the grill gates which were introduced before.

From the aesthetic point of view, the most interesting part is around the balconies. The style and decorations are usually copied by the window gratings.

They can stand in line with the facade or can reach out beyond the facade. And therefore they have been nominated as "kneeling rails".

They are used to provide a best view from exterior for the people who are standing in front of it.

Gratings

The specific definition of "kneeled" is determined by its appearance. This type of grating has bulges that give rise to the letter "S".

These gratings in particular prefer wavy and sinuous lines of Baroque Age. At that moment, the sinuosity of the shapes was intensified and extended to the upstairs balconies for the esthetic purpose.

In addition to the different appearances in different historical period, the gratings are also different in regions where they were designed and forged.

In Umbria the characteristics of balconies are "kneeled", while in Milan and its surroundings prevails "Spanish" style, from a more linear shape to a shape of pergola which was popular in Spain in 17th century.

In this century the balcony begins to decorate the facade of the buildings in a special way after a so-called "noble floor" style was introduced.

Gratings

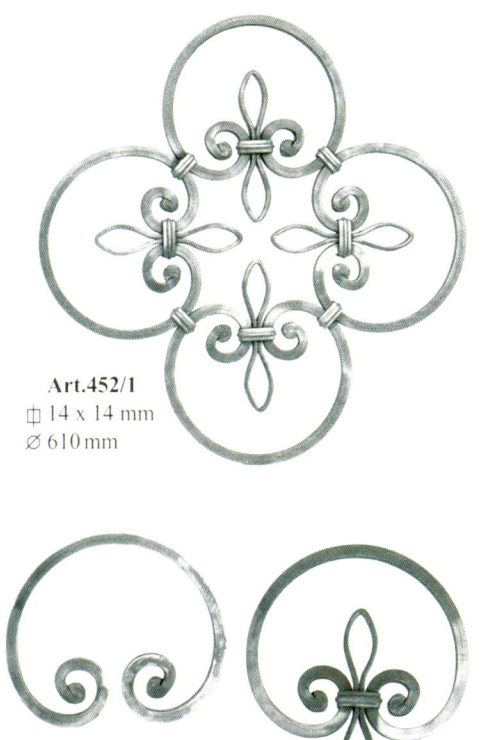

Art. 452/1
⊡ 14 x 14 mm
⌀ 610 mm

Art. 452/2
⊡ 14 x 14 mm
⌀ 265 x 220 mm

Art. 452/3
⊡ 14 x 14 mm
265 x 280 mm

Produzione: ind.i.a. SPA

071

Gratings

Art. 471/2
◨ 14 x 8 mm
250 x 425 mm

Art. 471/3
◨ 14 x 8 mm
125 x 425 mm

Gratings

There is a balcony which is larger than other balconies in the whole building and placed over the main gate, which is certainly decorated. The main function of the balcony in the "noble floor" is originally used to highlight the importance of the building: in fact the hosts live on the 1st floor and the servants live on the upstairs.

The gratings of the balcony belonging to the noble floor are usually full of decorations in a special way in the period of Baroque Age.

In compared with Baroque motifs, the liberty style prefers an oriental taste and floral themes for the most part.

The iron often adopts the complexity of shapes realized by blacksmith of liberty style, as it can be molded more easily while maintaining an appearance of lightness of the decorations.

The value of gratings lies in giving lightness to a too massive and heavy structure by virtue of the transparency that it could realize like a screen. In fact a metal grating offers the possibility of enriching the architectural ensembles with various decorative themes without risking weighing it down.

073

Gratings

Barre standard di L 2000 mm ca
Pierced bar length L 2000 mm ca

Produzione: ind.i.a. SPA

Gratings

Even the gratings inside the houses are a great example of many uses which the iron could have, combining always the practical function with decorative and ornamental function.

The railings dating from the late 19th century are present in Milan and were forged in the workshop of the master Mazzucotelli. So they convey a great artistic and architectural value.

The motifs are always those typical flowers of liberty style, while the form is twisted softly along the stairs as if they accompany the stairs.

Unfortunately, even in this case there are few samples that have come down to us. But today many metal railings are forged.

Naturally, the style and fashion have changed in favor of a certain practicality and sobriety of forms, but they also refer to liberty or Baroque with presence of such twisted decorations.

Gratings

Art. 657/2
□ 12 x 12 mm
260 x 400 mm

Art. 657/3
□ 12 x 12 mm
260 x 430 mm

Produzione: ind.i.a. SPA

076

Gratings

Art. 448/1
□ 8 x 8 mm
⌀ 435 mm

Produzione: ind.i.a. SPA

Gratings

Gratings

Gratings

★ Art. 595/1
⌀ 12 mm
H 900 mm

★ Art. 595/2
⌀ 14 mm
H 900 mm

★ Art. 595/3
⌀ 16 mm
H 900 mm

★ Art. 595/4
⌀ 18 mm
H 900 mm

★ Art. 595/16
▢ 12 x 12 mm
H 900 mm

★ Art. 595/17
▢ 14 x 14 mm
H 900 mm

Art. 595/5
▢ 20 x 20 mm
H 1100 mm

Produzione: ind.i.a. SPA

080

Gratings

Art. 594/1	Art. 594/2	Art. 594/3
☐ 14 x 14 mm	☐ 14 x 14 mm	☐ 14 x 14 mm
H 1100 mm	H 1100 mm	H 1100 mm

Produzione: ind.i.a. SPA

Gratings

Gratings

Barre di lunghezza 3000 mm
Length of bar 3000 mm

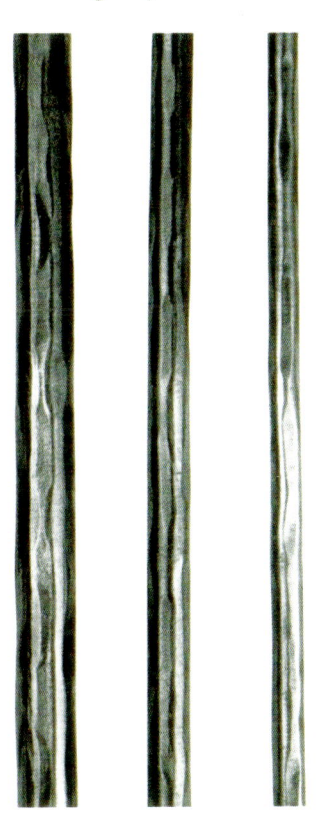

Produzione: ind.i.a. SPA

Gratings

Produzione: ind.i.a. SPA

084

Gratings

Art. 114/9
◇ 30 x 8 mm
L 3000 mm

Art. 158/26
◇ 12 x 6 mm
x 2 barre - bars

Art. 38/2
◇ 12 x 6 mm
D 80 per mm
240 mm Passo
H 1600 mm

Passo
Pitch

Produzione: ind.i.a. SPA

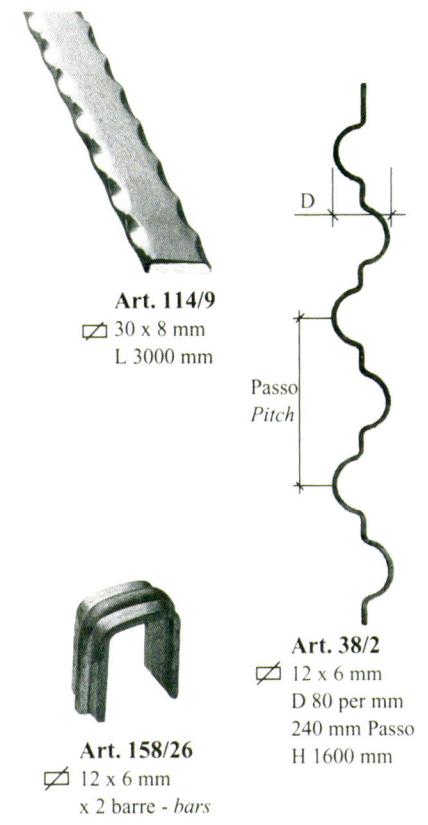

085

Gratings

Art. 51/3
□ 12 x 12 mm
300 x 900 mm

Art. 53/3
□ 12 x 12 mm
H 900 mm

Art. 114/9
◊ 30 x 8 mm
L 3000 mm

Produzione: ind.i.a. SPA

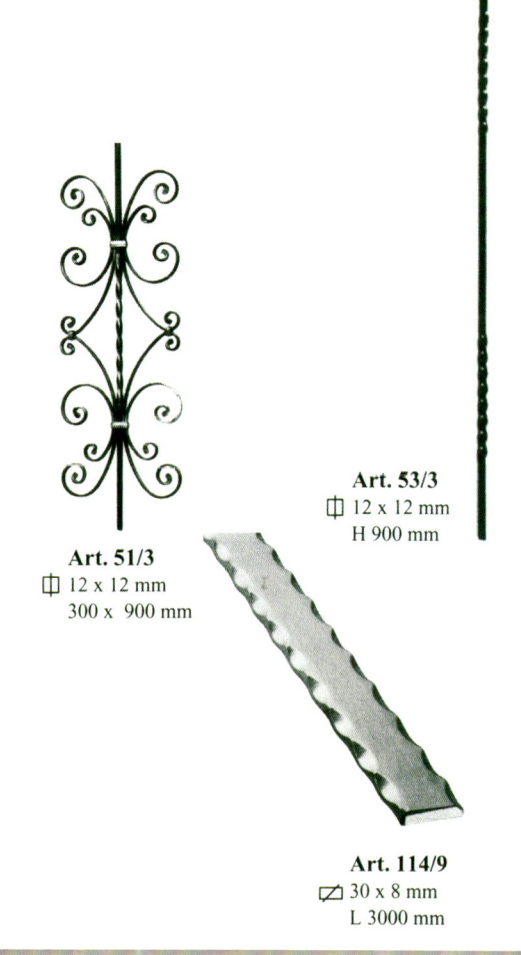

Gratings

Gratings

Art. 659/10
⌀ 12 mm
80 x 130 mm

Art. 810/A/10
30 x 10 mm
L 6000 mm

Art. 158/1
14 x 14 mm
L 4000 mm

Art. 1361/6
14 x 14 mm
150 mm Inter. - *Pitch*
13 fori per barra - *holes*

Produzione: ind.i.a. SPA

Gratings

Art. 1043/2
☐ 12 x 12 mm
490 x 1030 mm

Art. 78/B/3
☐ 12 x 12 mm
110 x 300 mm

Art. 1043/1
☐ 12 x 12 mm
210 x 1030 mm

Produzione: ind.i.a. SPA

Gratings

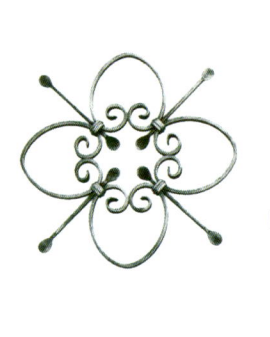

Art. 1299/2
12 x 6 mm
140 x 140 mm

Art. 1009/2
12 x 6 mm
Ø 370 mm

Art. 117/2
Ø 20 mm

Art. 117/6
Ø 40 mm

Art. 852/4
8 mm
124 x 1190 mm

Art. 852/8
6 mm
70 x 1140 mm

Produzione: ind.i.a. SPA

Gratings

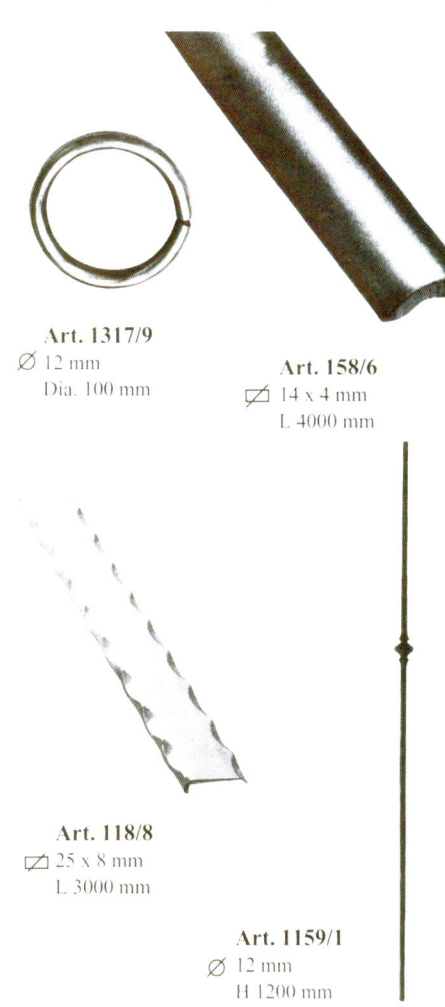

Art. 1317/9
⌀ 12 mm
Dia. 100 mm

Art. 158/6
◇ 14 x 4 mm
L 4000 mm

Art. 118/8
◇ 25 x 8 mm
L 3000 mm

Art. 1159/1
⌀ 12 mm
H 1200 mm

Produzione: ind.i.a. SPA

Gratings

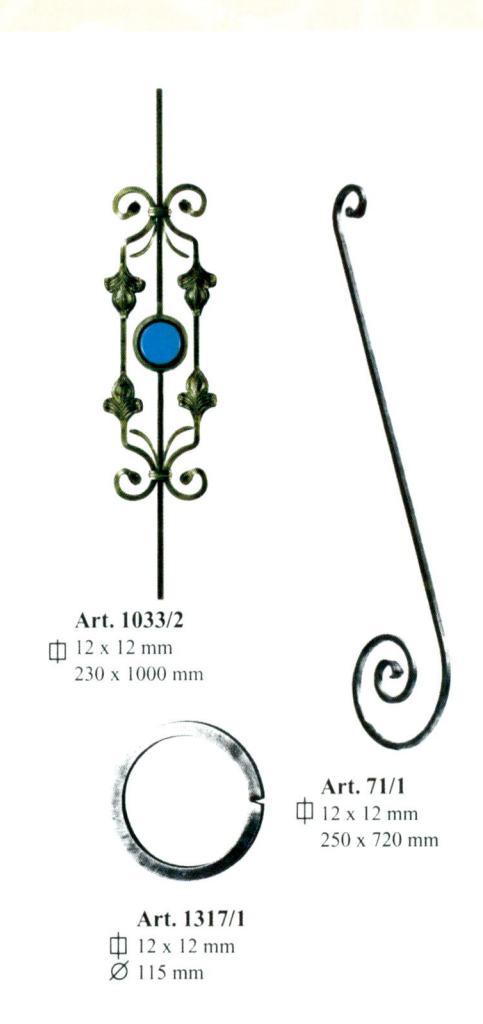

Art. 1033/2
⬜ 12 x 12 mm
230 x 1000 mm

Art. 71/1
⬜ 12 x 12 mm
250 x 720 mm

Art. 1317/1
⬜ 12 x 12 mm
⌀ 115 mm

Produzione: ind.i.a. SPA

Gratings

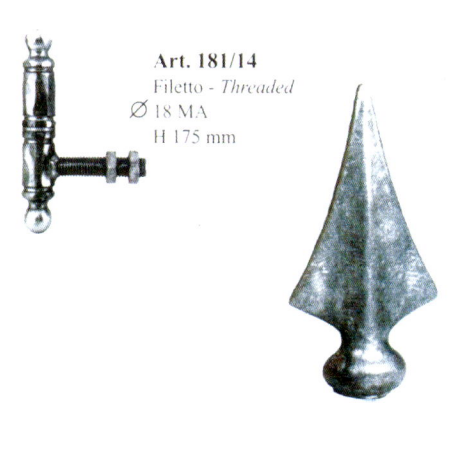

Art. 181/14
Filetto - *Threaded*
Ø 18 MA
H 175 mm

Art. 125/1
Base
Ø 35 mm
L 125 mm

Art. 6258/2
25 x 6 mm
L 3000 mm

Produzione: ind.i.a. SPA

Gratings

Art. 1279/2
20 x 20 mm
285 x 340 mm

Art. 1231/2
Ø 30 mm Tubo - *Tube*
H 1000 mm

Art. 1279/4
20 x 6 mm
235 x 720 mm

Produzione: ind.i.a. SPA

Gratings

Art. 1034/2
□ 12 x 12 mm
230 x 1000 mm

Art. 71/1
□ 12 x 12 mm
250 x 720 mm

Art. 1317/1
□ 12 x 12 mm
Ø 115 mm

Art. 160/H/N
Ø 97 mm

Produzione: ind.i.a. SPA

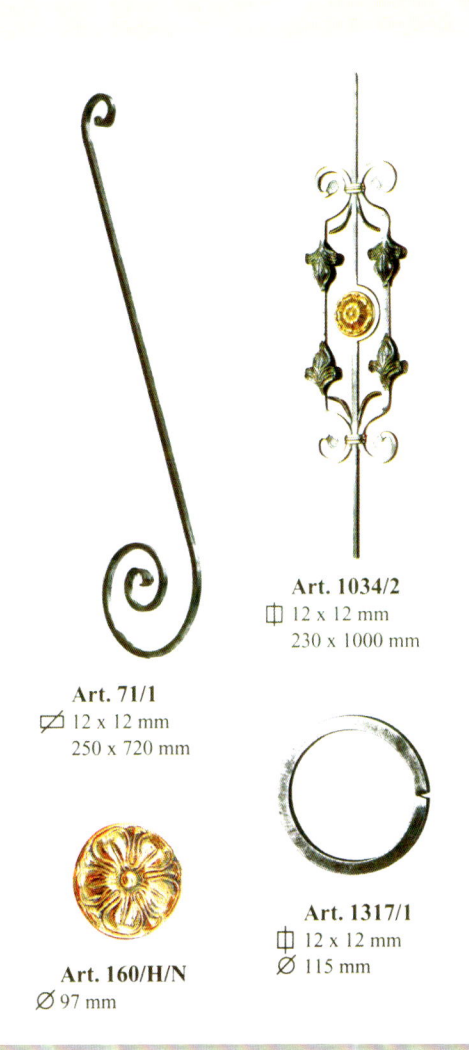

Gratings

Art. 745/1
⌀ 97 mm

Art. 1035/2
☐ 12 x 12 mm
230 x 1000 mm

Art. 118/A/6
◇ 30 x 8 mm
L 3000 mm

Art. 71/1
◇ 12 x 12 mm
250 x 720 mm

Produzione: ind.i.a. SPA

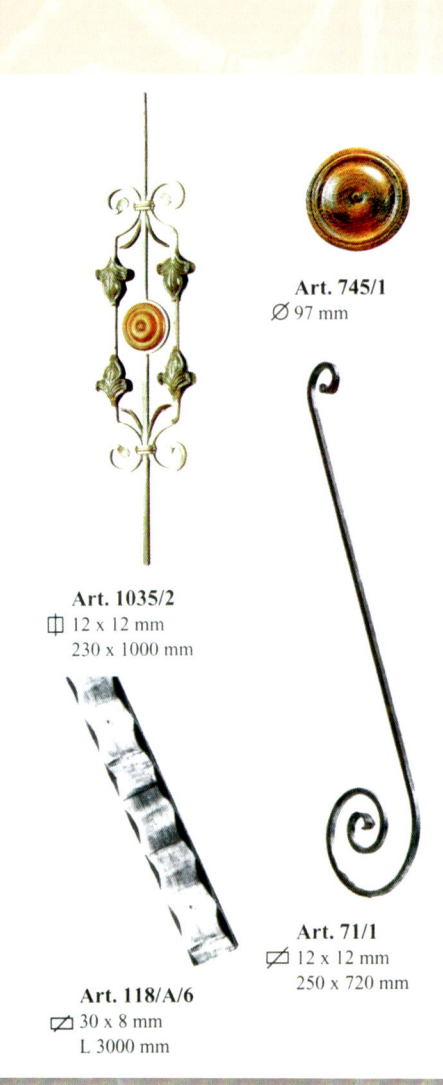

Gratings

Art. 118/A/7
30 x 10 mm
L 3000 mm

Art. 1358/4
12 x 12 mm
H 1600 mm

118/1
12 x 12 mm
L 3000 mm

Art. 116/A/4
3 mm
Ø 65 mm

Produzione: ind.i.a. SPA

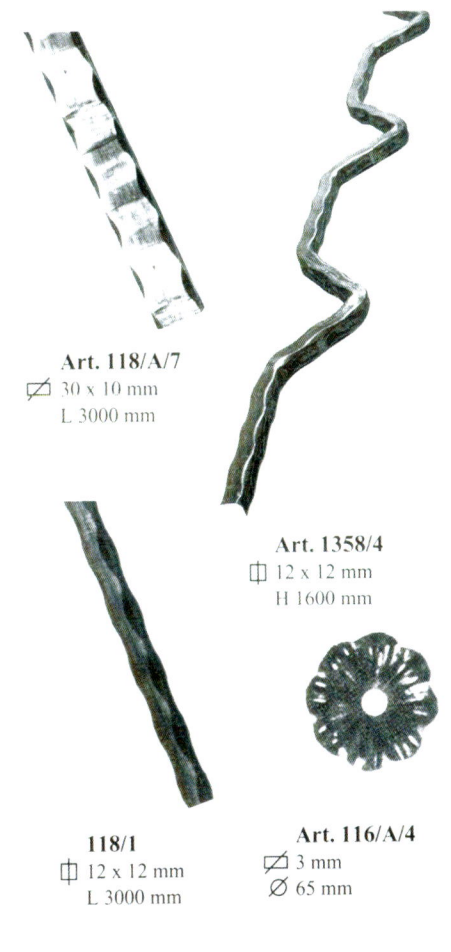

Gratings

Gratings

Art. 114/8
◱ 40 x 8 mm
L. 3000 mm

Art. 114/9
◱ 30 x 8 mm
L. 3000 mm

Art. 596/3
⌀ 12 mm
250 x 900 mm

Produzione: ind.i.a. SPA

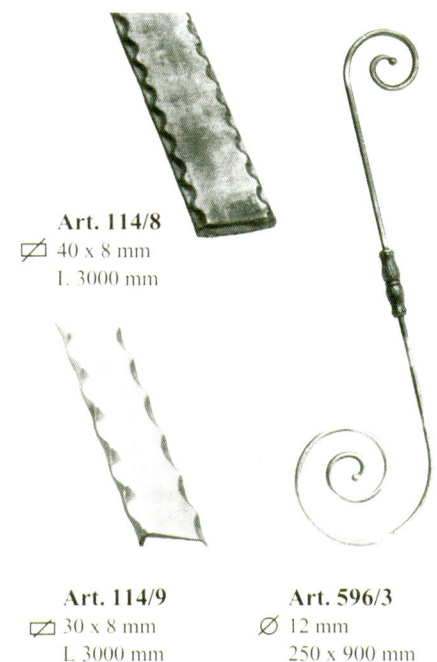

Gratings

Gratings

Art. 1032/2
⬜ 12 x 12 mm
230 x 1000 mm

Art. 491/8
⬜ 12 x 12 mm
⌀ 100 mm
Liscio - *Plain*

Produzione: ind.i.a. SPA

Gratings

Art. 611/8
☐ 14 x 14 mm
L 810 mm
5 borchiatura - *hammering*

Art. 47/3
☐ 12 x 12 mm
H 900 mm

14 x 4 mm

Art. 158/28
▱ 12 x 6 mm x 4 barre - *bars*

Art. 80/A/1
▱ 12 x 6 mm

Produzione: ind.i.a. SPA

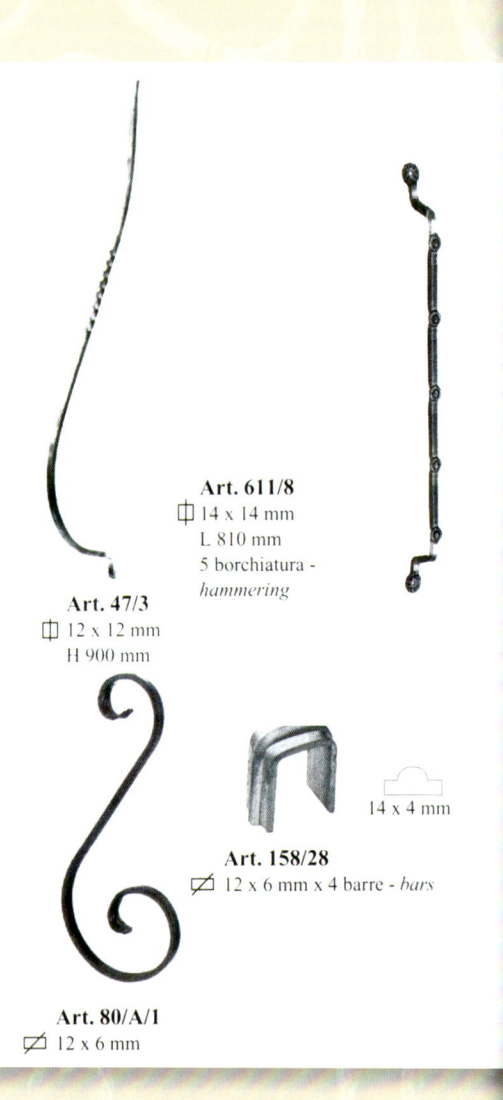

Gratings

Art. 85/8
L 25 mm Fascetta - *Collar*
12 x 12 mm x 2 barre - *bars*

18 x 5 mm

Art. 24/3
⌑ 12 x 12 mm
Ø 600 mm

Produzione: ind.i.a. SPA

103

Gratings

Art. 114/A/6
◫ 17 x 58 mm
L 3000 mm

Art. 114/A/1
◫ 43 x 7 mm
L 3700 mm

Art. 1075/1
⌀ 10 mm
245 x 1000 mm

Art. 1368/8
⌀ 10 mm
L 3000 mm

Art. 114/9
◫ 30 x 8 mm
L 3000 mm

Produzione: ind.i.a. SPA

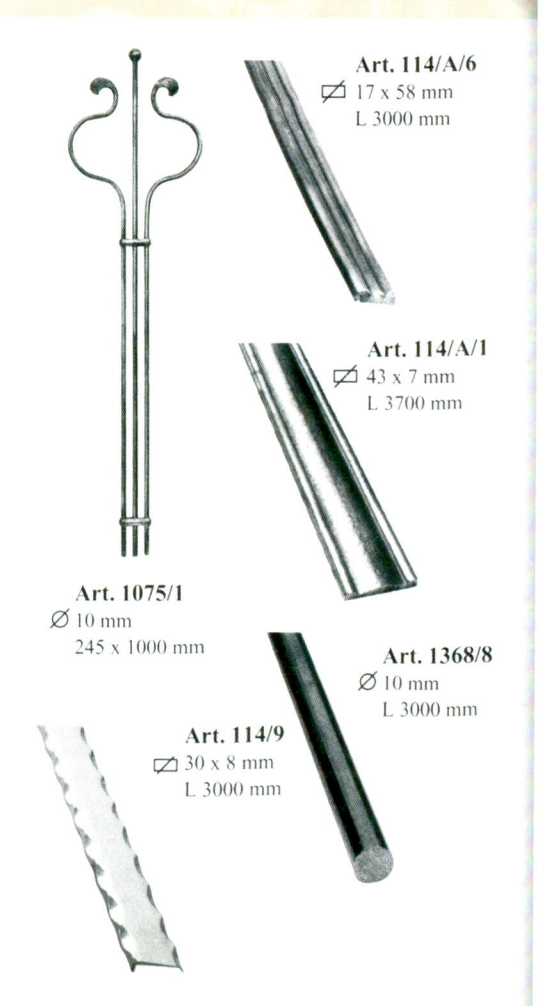

104

Gratings

Art. 1012/1
⌀ 12 mm
Dia. 560 mm

Art. 1054/5
⌀ 12 mm
210 x 1000 mm

Art. 158/10
⌀ 30 x 8 mm
L. 3500 mm

Produzione: ind.i.a. SPA

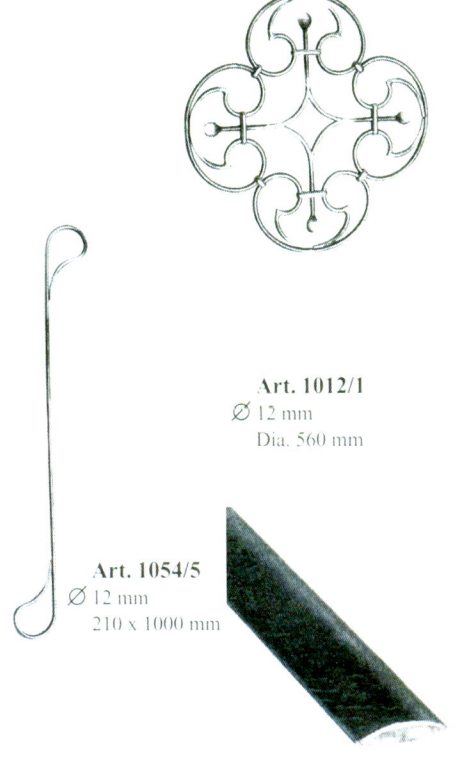

Gratings

Art. 116/A/4
◻ 3 mm
Ø 65 mm

Art. 447/1
Ø 14 mm
Dia. 620 mm

Art. 634/6
Ø 14 mm
220 x 300 mm

Art. 158/6
Ø 14 x 4 mm
L 4000 mm

Produzione: ind.i.a. SPA

Gratings

Art. 1279/2
⊡ 20 x 20 mm
285 x 340 mm

Art. 1170/1
⌀ 12 mm
130 x 1000 mm

Art. 1279/4
▱ 20 x 6 mm
235 x 720 mm

Produzione: ind.i.a. SPA

Gratings

Art. 810/A/2
⌀ 35 x 10 mm
L 3000 mm

Art. 1231/2
⌀ 30 mm Tubo - *Tube*
H 1000 mm

Produzione: ind.i.a. SPA

Gratings

Gratings

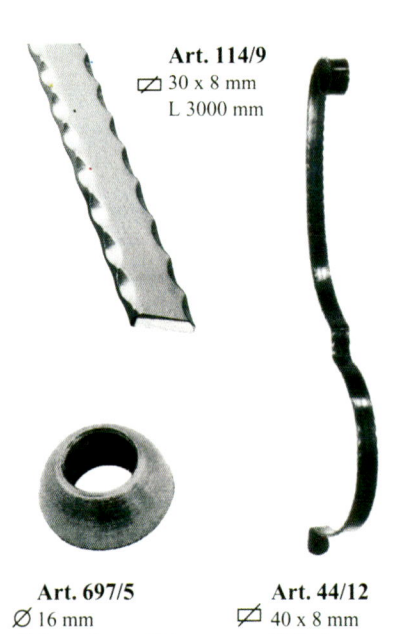

Art. 114/9
◻ 30 x 8 mm
L 3000 mm

Art. 697/5
⌀ 16 mm
⌀ 8 mm Foro - *Hole*

Art. 44/12
◻ 40 x 8 mm
H 1000 mm

Produzione: ind.i.a. SPA

Gratings

Art. 125/2
14 mm base
H 140 mm

Art. 88/H/3
12 x 6 mm
75 x 130 mm

Produzione: ind.i.a. SPA

Gratings

Gratings

Art. 118/A/7
◻ 30 x 10 mm
L 3000 mm

Art. 109/2
◻ 60 x 8 mm
H 1000 mm

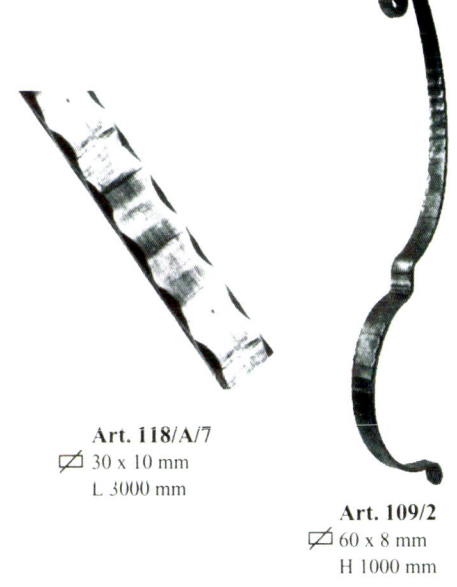

Art. 697/5
⌀ 16 mm
⌀ 8 mm Foro - *Hole*

Produzione: ind.i.a. SPA

113

Gratings

Art. 1281/3
16 x 8 mm
830 x 340 mm

Art. 40/A/1
12 x 12 mm
L 6000 mm
140 mm Inter. - *Pitch*

Produzione: ind.i.a. SPA

114

Gratings

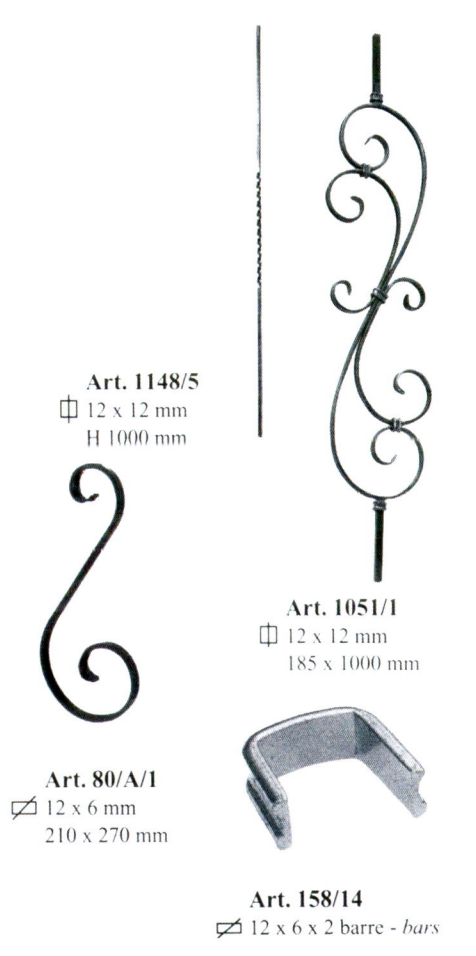

Art. 1148/5
⊡ 12 x 12 mm
H 1000 mm

Art. 1051/1
⊡ 12 x 12 mm
185 x 1000 mm

Art. 80/A/1
⌀ 12 x 6 mm
210 x 270 mm

Art. 158/14
⌀ 12 x 6 x 2 barre - *bars*

Produzione: ind.i.a. SPA

Gratings

Art. 1028/2
◻ 12 x 12 mm
⌀ 630 mm

Art. 491/8
◻ 12 x 12 mm
⌀ 100 mm
Liscio - *Plain*

Art. 85/8
18 x 5 mm
Fascetta L 25 mm
Collar 25 mm
◻ 12 x 12 x 2 barre - *bars*

Art. 85/9
Fascetta L 37 mm
Collar 37 mm
◻ 12 x 12 x 2 barre - *bars*

Produzione: ind.i.a. SPA

Gratings

Gratings

Art. 114/9
◻ 30 x 8 mm
L 3000 mm

D
Passo
Pitch

Art. 38/2
◻ 12 x 6 mm
D 80 mm
Passo - *Pitch* 250 mm

14 x 4 mm

Art. 158/26
◻ 12 x 6 mm
x 2 barre - *bars*

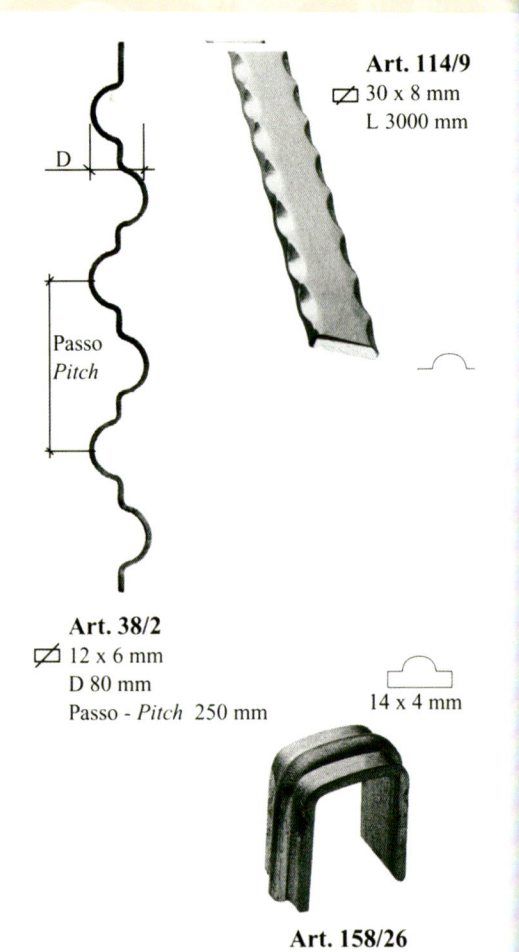

Produzione: ind.i.a. SPA

Gratings

Art. 65/8
⊡ 12 x 12 mm
H 900 mm

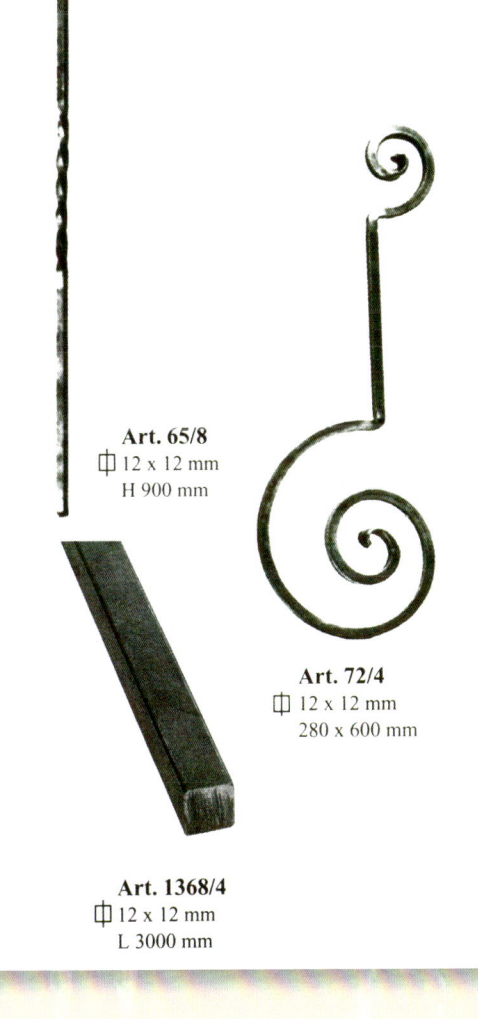

Art. 72/4
⊡ 12 x 12 mm
280 x 600 mm

Art. 1368/4
⊡ 12 x 12 mm
L 3000 mm

Produzione: ind.i.a. SPA

Gratings

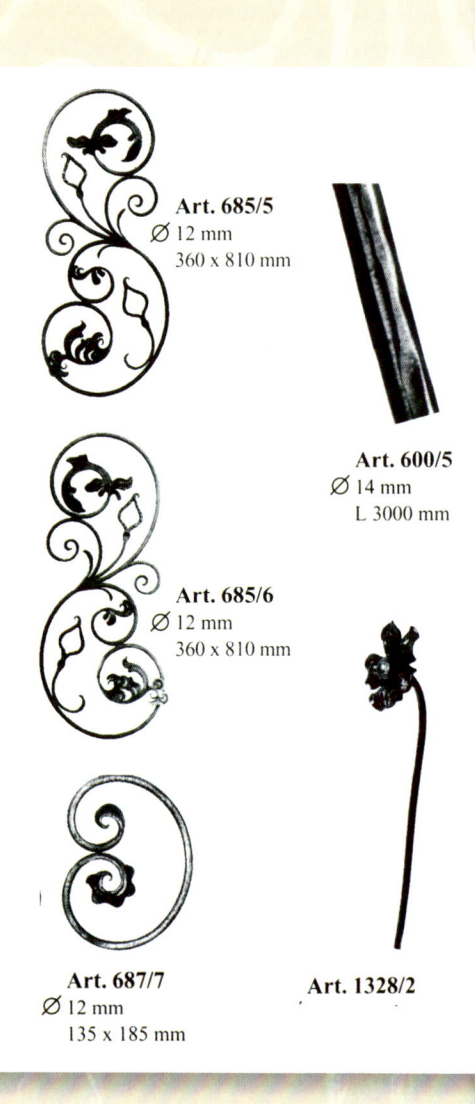

Art. 685/5
Ø 12 mm
360 x 810 mm

Art. 600/5
Ø 14 mm
L 3000 mm

Art. 685/6
Ø 12 mm
360 x 810 mm

Art. 1328/2

Art. 687/7
Ø 12 mm
135 x 185 mm

Produzione: ind.i.a. SPA

Gratings

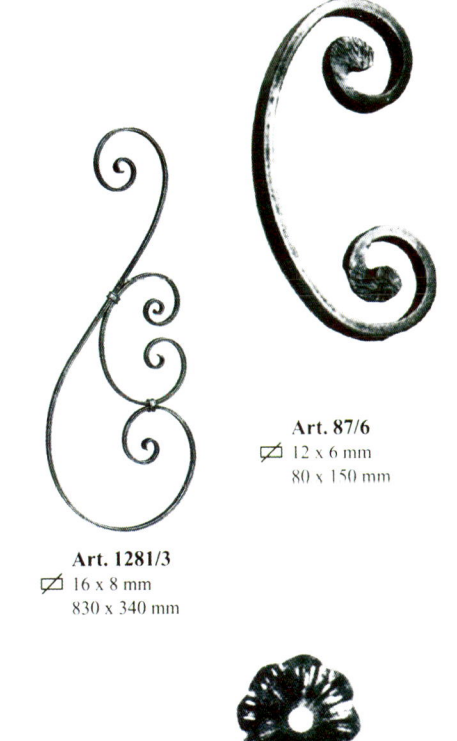

Art. 87/6
◻ 12 x 6 mm
80 x 150 mm

Art. 1281/3
◻ 16 x 8 mm
830 x 340 mm

Art. 116/A/4
◻ 3 mm
⌀ 65 mm

Produzione: ind.i.a. SPA

Gratings

Art. 78/B/1
12 x 12 mm
110 x 220 mm

Art. 78/B/2
12 x 12 mm
110 x 220 mm

Art. 116/E/3
20 x 8 mm
300 x 800 mm

Produzione: ind.i.a. SPA

Gratings

Art. 114/9
30 x 8 mm
L 3000 mm

Art. 1014/3
sfere vuote-*hollow*　Ø 12 mm
spheres DIA 30 mm　DIA 290 mm

Produzione: ind.i.a. SPA

Gratings

Gratings

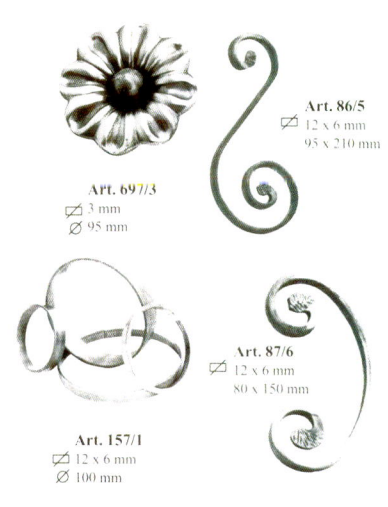

Art. 697/3
◻ 3 mm
⌀ 95 mm

Art. 86/5
◻ 12 x 6 mm
95 x 210 mm

Art. 157/1
◻ 12 x 6 mm
⌀ 100 mm

Art. 87/6
◻ 12 x 6 mm
80 x 150 mm

Produzione: ind.i.a. SPA

Art. 140/B/2
◻ 5 mm
165 x 140 mm

Art. 116/A/4
◻ 3 mm
⌀ 65 mm

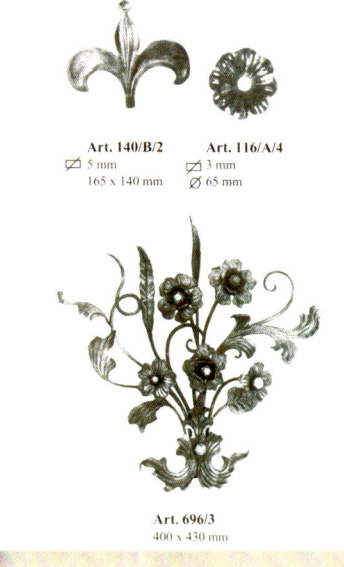

Art. 696/3
400 x 430 mm

125

Gratings

Art. 24/3
⬜ 12 x 12 mm
⌀ 600 mm

Art. 114/9
◇ 30 x 8 mm
L 3000 mm

18 x 5 mm
Art. 85/8
⬜ 12 x 12 mm x 2 barre - *bars*
L 25 mm
Fascetta - *Collar*

Produzione: ind.i.a. SPA

126

Gratings

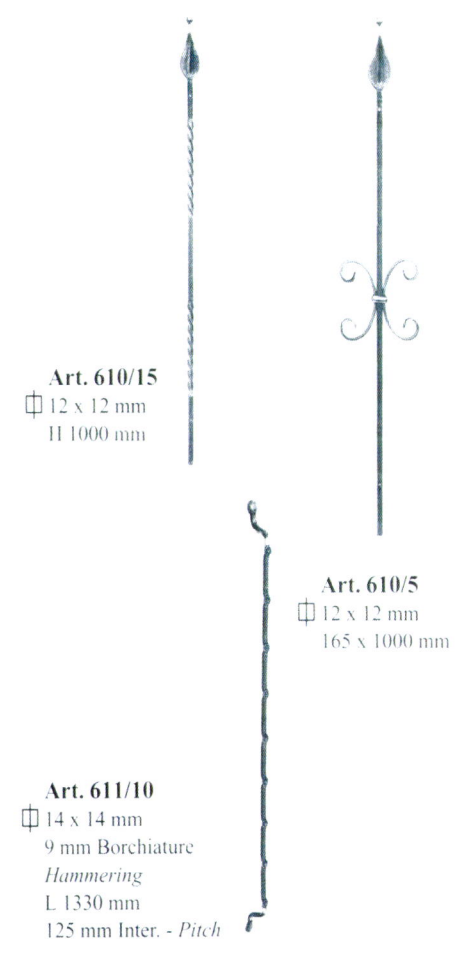

Art. 610/15
☐ 12 x 12 mm
H 1000 mm

Art. 610/5
☐ 12 x 12 mm
165 x 1000 mm

Art. 611/10
☐ 14 x 14 mm
9 mm Borchiature
Hammering
L 1330 mm
125 mm Inter. - *Pitch*

Produzione: ind.i.a. SPA

Gratings

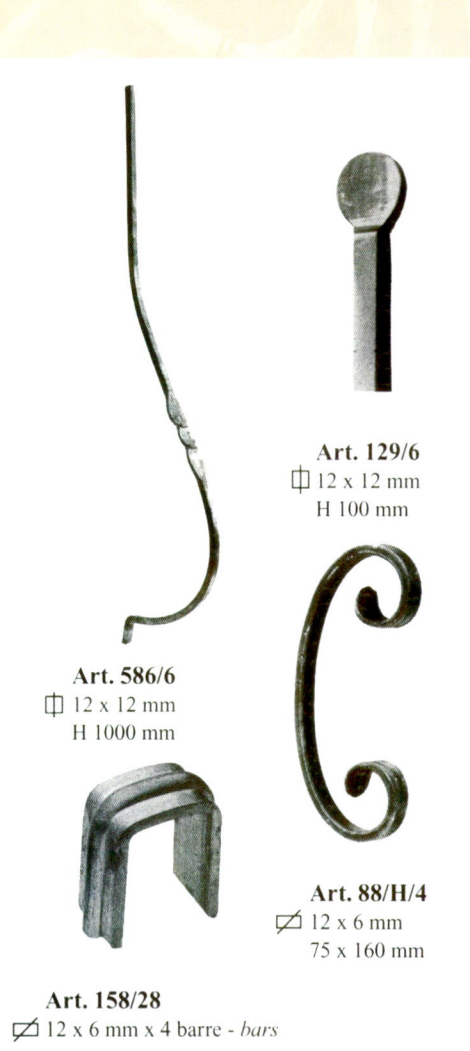

Art. 129/6
◻ 12 x 12 mm
H 100 mm

Art. 586/6
◻ 12 x 12 mm
H 1000 mm

Art. 88/H/4
▱ 12 x 6 mm
75 x 160 mm

Art. 158/28
▱ 12 x 6 mm x 4 barre - bars

Produzione: ind.i.a. SPA

Gratings

Art. 510/1
▫ 12 x 12 mm
250 x 900 mm

Produzione: ind.i.a. SPA

129

Gratings

Gratings

Art. 158/48
⌀ 50 x 10 mm

Art.476/1
☐ 12 x 12 mm
380 x 900 mm

Art. 116/F/3
⌀ 30 mm

Art. 697/4
◊ 3 mm
⌀ 65 mm

Art. 479/1
☐ 12 x 12 mm
110 x 900 mm

Produzione: ind.i.a. SPA

131

Gratings

Art. 474/1
12 x 12 mm
380 x 755 mm

Produzione: ind.i.a. SPA

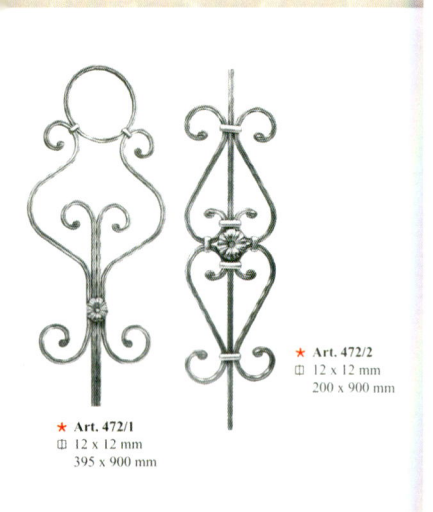

★ **Art. 472/2**
12 x 12 mm
200 x 900 mm

★ **Art. 472/1**
12 x 12 mm
395 x 900 mm

Gratings

133

Gratings

Produzione: ind.i.a. SPA

Gratings

Produzione: ind.i.a. SPA

135

Gratings

Art. 571/3
⏥ 12 x 12 mm
200 x 900 mm
H 900 mm

Art. 571/4
⏥ 14 x 14 mm
H 900 mm

Produzione: ind.i.a. SPA

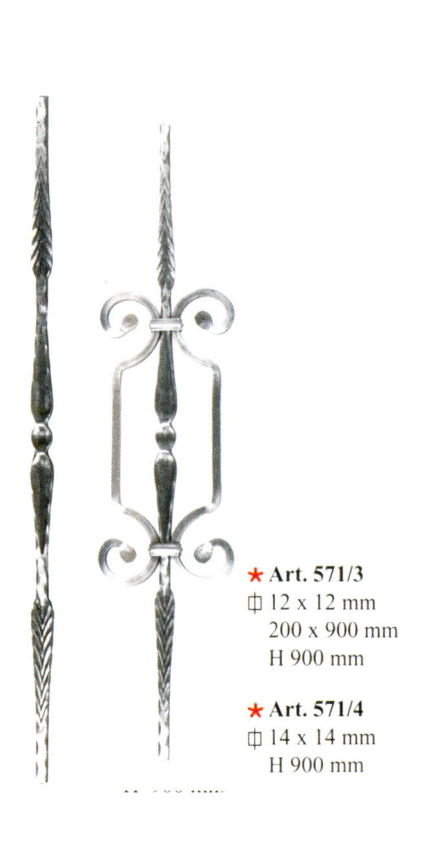

Gratings

Gratings

Art.73/1
☐ 8 x 8 mm
110 x 300 mm

Art.73/3
☐ 8 x 8 mm
90 x 180 mm

Art.451/1
☐ 8 x 8 mm
Ø 575 mm

Produzione: ind.i.a. SPA

Gratings

Art. 715/2
⌀ 12 mm
martellato
hammered
580 x H 880 mm

Produzione: ind.i.a. SPA

Art. 457/1
□ 12 x 6 mm
1020 x 1020 mm

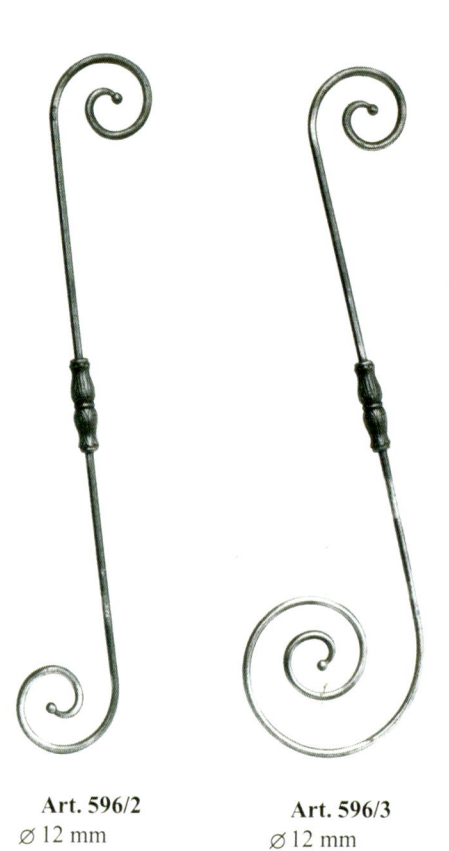

Gratings

Art. 596/2
⌀ 12 mm
150 x 900 mm

Art. 596/3
⌀ 12 mm
250 x 900 mm

Produzione: ind.i.a. SPA

Gratings

Tondo
Round

Art. 572/1
⌀ 12 mm
H 900 mm

Art. 572/2
⌀ 12 mm
H 1200 mm

Art. 572/3
⌀ 14 mm
H 900 mm

Art. 572/4
⌀ 14 mm
H 1200 mm

Produzione: ind.i.a. SPA

Gratings

Art. 584/4
⌑ 12 x 12 mm
165 x 900 mm

Art. 584/5
⌑ 12 x 12 mm
165 x 900 mm

Produzione: ind.i.a. SPA

Gratings

Art.456/1
◻ 12 x 12 mm
400 x 1020 mm

Art.456/3
◇ 12 x 6 mm
545 x 1020 mm

Produzione: ind.i.a. SPA

143

Gratings

Art. 604/4
⌀16 mm
H 250 mm

Art. 604/9
⌀12 mm
H 250 mm

Produzione: ind.i.a. SPA

Gratings

Art. 604/1
⌀16 mm
H 1000 mm

Art. 604/2
⌀16 mm
H 1000 mm

Art. 604/6
⌀12 mm
H 1000 mm

Art. 604/7
⌀12 mm
H 1000 mm

Produzione: ind.i.a. SPA

Gratings

Art. 504/1
⌀ 12 mm
H 1000 mm

Produzione: ind.i.a. SPA

146

Gratings

Art. 1360/2
◻ 14 x 14 mm
int. - *pitch* 140 mm
n° fori - *holes* 14
L 2000 mm

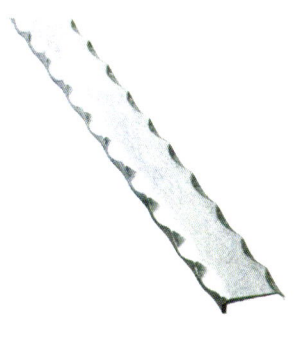

Art. 114/9
▱ 30 x 8 mm
L 3000 mm

Produzione: ind.i.a. SPA

Gratings

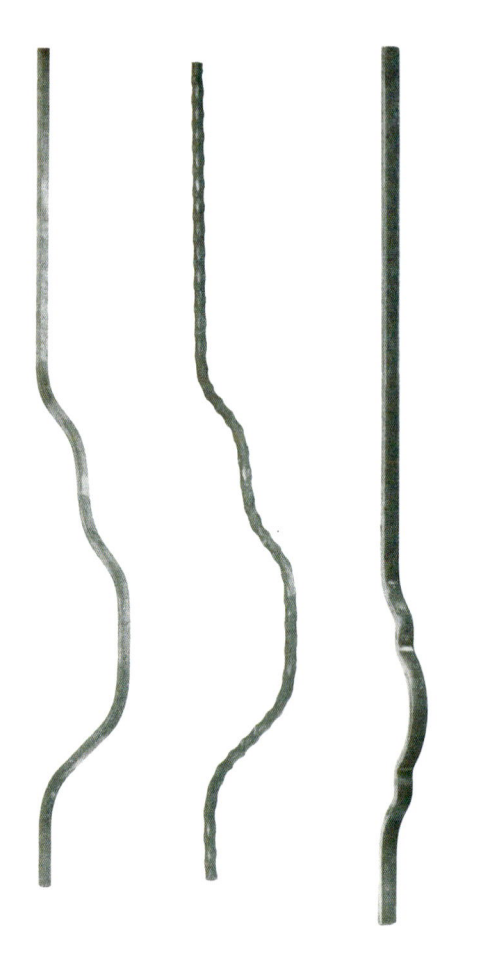

Produzione: ind.i.a. SPA

Gratings

Art. 116/A/4
◻ 3 mm
⌀ 65 mm

Art. 116/A/5
⌀ 95 mm

Art. 697/1 / 3002/17
90 mm ◻ 3 mm

Art. 697/2
60 mm - ◻ 3 mm

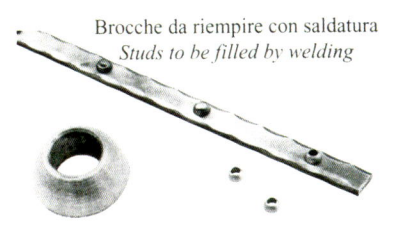

Art. 697/4
◻ 3 mm
⌀ 65 mm

Brocche da riempire con saldatura
Studs to be filled by welding

Art. 697/5
⌀ 16 mm
Foro - *Hole*
⌀ 8 mm

Produzione: ind.i.a. SPA

Gratings

Gratings

Art. 491/8
☐ 12 mm
Ø 100 mm
Liscio - Plain

Art. 1045/4
☐ 12 x 12 mm
265 x 1000 mm

780 mm

Art. 85/8
L 25 mm
Art. 85/9
L 37 mm
Fascetta - Collar

Art. 94/P/1
☐ 12 x 12 mm
105 x 220 mm

Produzione: ind.i.a. SPA

Gratings

Art. 1368/9
⌀ 12 mm
L 3000 mm

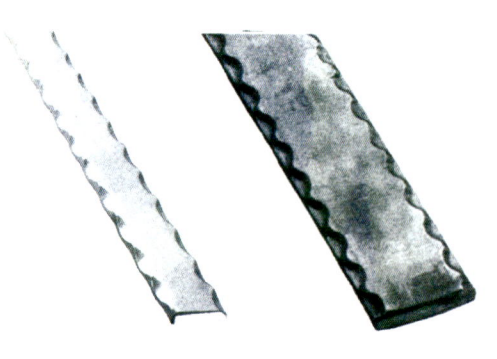

Art. 114/9
◇ 30 x 8 mm
L 3000 mm

Art. 114/8
◇ 40 x 8 mm
L 3000 mm

Produzione: ind.i.a. SPA

152

Gratings

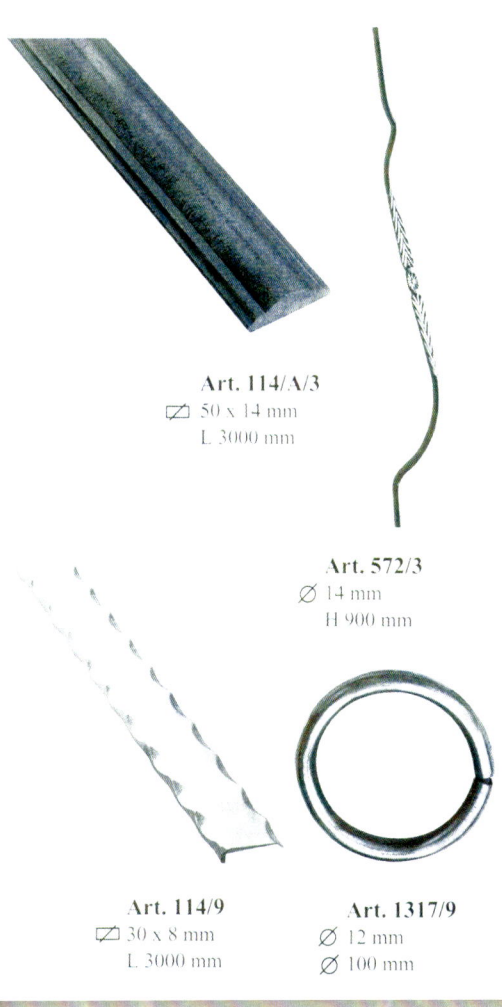

Art. 114/A/3
◻ 50 x 14 mm
L 3000 mm

Art. 572/3
∅ 14 mm
H 900 mm

Art. 114/9
◻ 30 x 8 mm
L 3000 mm

Art. 1317/9
∅ 12 mm
∅ 100 mm

Produzione: ind.i.a. SPA

Gratings

Tubo di acciaio
rigato Ø 30 mm
*Steel tube
grooved
DIA 30 mm*

Art. 1231/3
Ø 30 mm
H 1000 mm

Art. 1236/1
113 x 1030 mm

Art. 1373/3
45 x 12 mm
L 3000 mm

Produzione: ind.i.a. SPA

154

Gratings

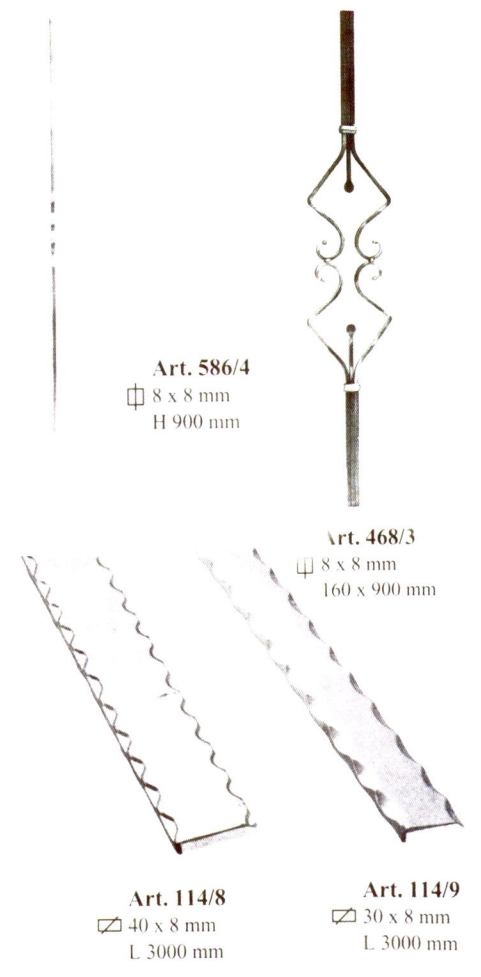

Art. 586/4
◻ 8 x 8 mm
H 900 mm

Art. 468/3
◻ 8 x 8 mm
160 x 900 mm

Art. 114/8
▱ 40 x 8 mm
L 3000 mm

Art. 114/9
▱ 30 x 8 mm
L 3000 mm

Produzione: ind.i.a. SPA

155

Gratings

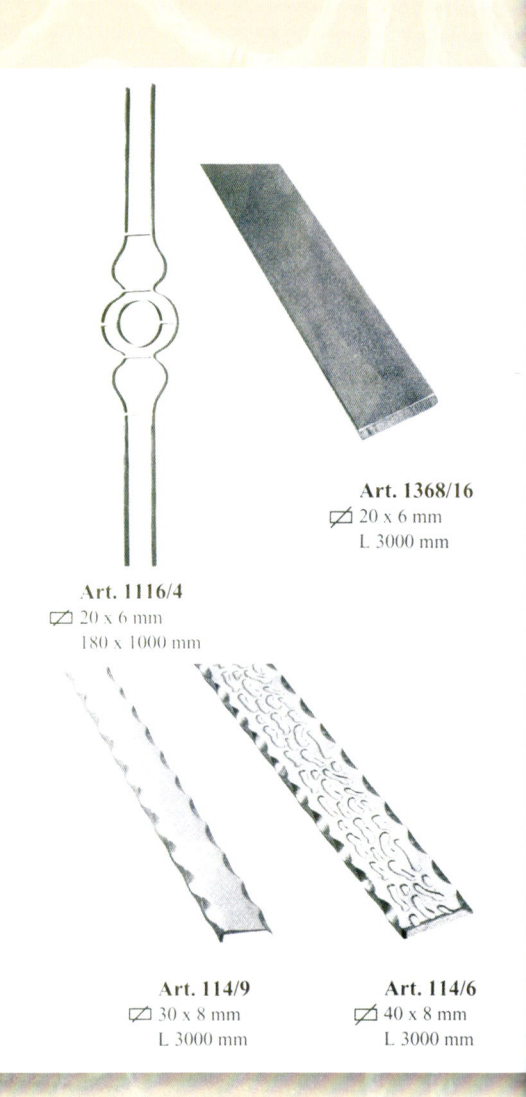

Art. 1116/4
◊ 20 x 6 mm
180 x 1000 mm

Art. 1368/16
◊ 20 x 6 mm
L 3000 mm

Art. 114/9
◊ 30 x 8 mm
L 3000 mm

Art. 114/6
◊ 40 x 8 mm
L 3000 mm

Produzione: ind.i.a. SPA

Gratings

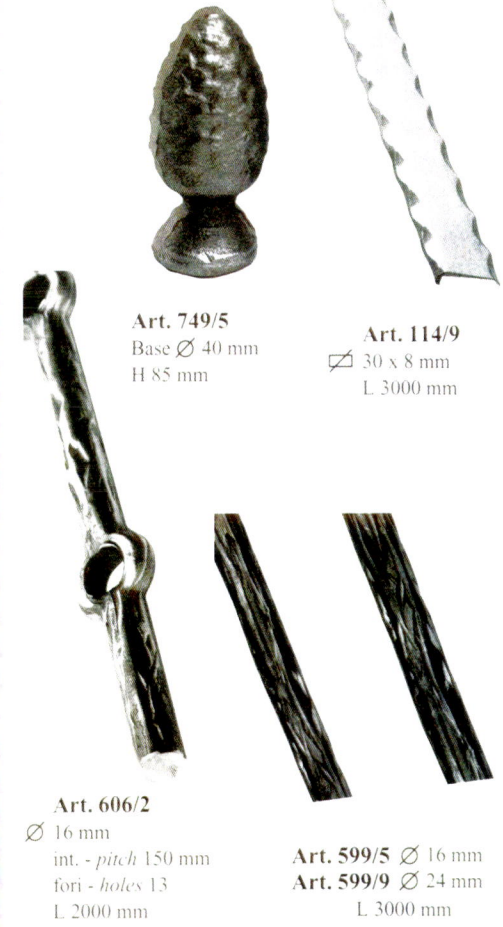

Art. 749/5
Base ⌀ 40 mm
H 85 mm

Art. 114/9
◇ 30 x 8 mm
L 3000 mm

Art. 606/2
⌀ 16 mm
int. - *pitch* 150 mm
fori - *holes* 13
L 2000 mm

Art. 599/5 ⌀ 16 mm
Art. 599/9 ⌀ 24 mm
L 3000 mm

Produzione: ind.i.a. SPA

Gratings

Art. 118/A/6
◻ 30 x 8 mm
L 3000 mm

Art. 750/1
⌀ 14 mm
H 125 mm

Art. 600/4
⌀ 12 mm
L 3000 mm

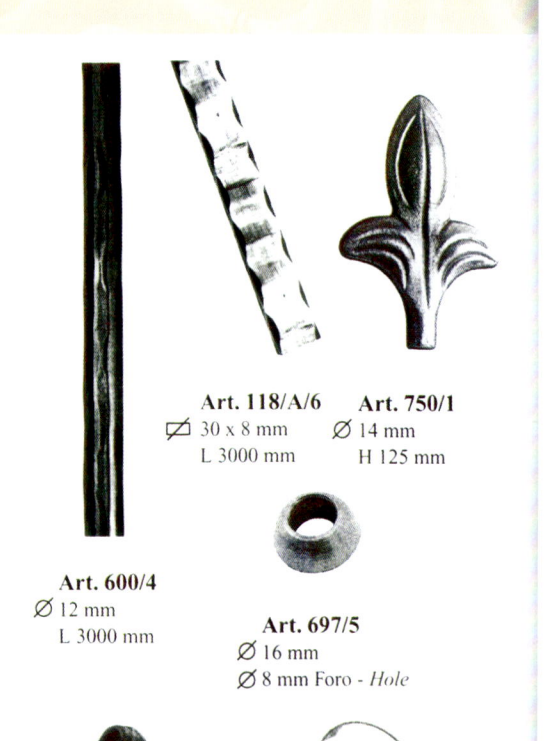

Art. 697/5
⌀ 16 mm
⌀ 8 mm Foro - Hole

Art. 80/A/3
◻ 12 x 6 mm
65 x 110 mm

Art. 157/2
◻ 12 x 6 mm
⌀ 115 mm

Produzione: ind.i.a. SPA

Gratings

Art. 158/28
4 barre - *bars*
12 x 6 mm

Art. 697/5
Ø 16 mm
Ø 8 mm Foro - *Hole*

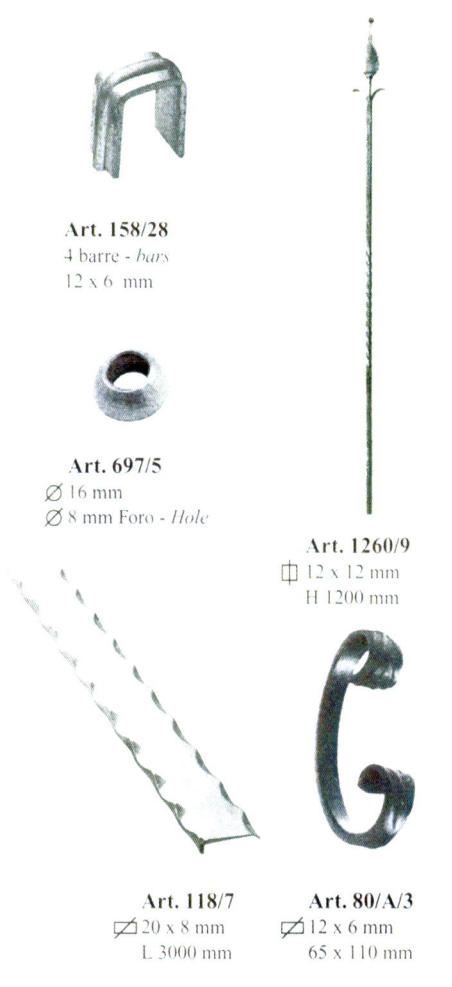

Art. 1260/9
☐ 12 x 12 mm
H 1200 mm

Art. 118/7
◇ 20 x 8 mm
L 3000 mm

Art. 80/A/3
◇ 12 x 6 mm
65 x 110 mm

Produzione: ind.i.a. SPA

Gratings

Art. 571/4
◻ 14 x 14 mm
H 900 mm

Art. 64/L/2
◻ 14 x 14 mm
H 900 mm

Art. 114/9
▱ 30 x 8 mm
L 3000 mm

Art. 114/8
▱ 40 x 8 mm
L 3000 mm

Produzione: ind.i.a. SPA

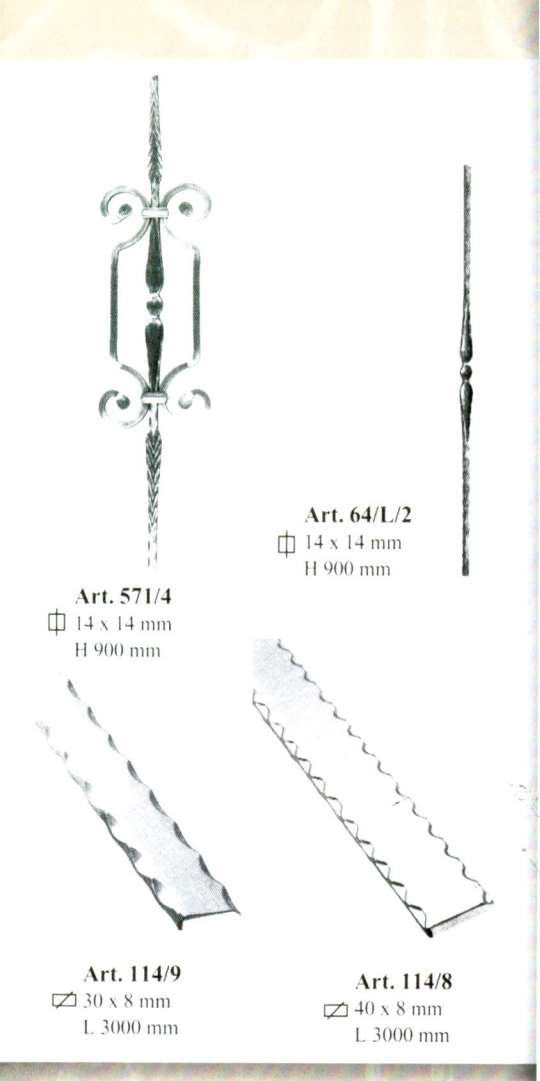

Gratings

Art. 598/1
Ø 12 mm
L 3000 mm

Art. 802/3
Ø 25 mm
Ø 35 base
H 1500 mm

Art. 810/A/12
Ø 40 x 10 mm
L 6000 mm

Produzione: ind.i.a. SPA

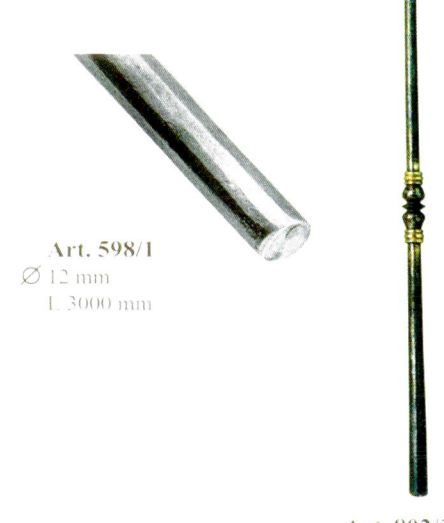

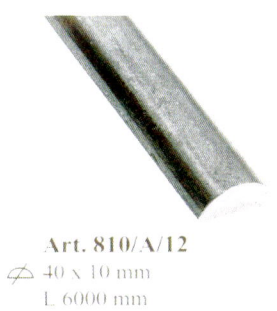

161

Gratings

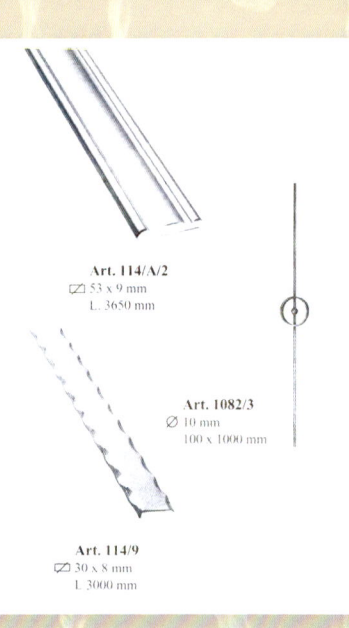

Art. 114/A/2
53 x 9 mm
L. 3650 mm

Art. 1082/3
⌀ 10 mm
100 x 1000 mm

Art. 114/9
30 x 8 mm
L. 3000 mm

Produzione: ind.i.a. SPA

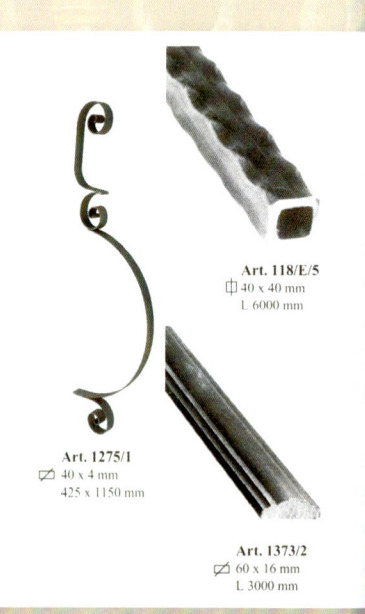

Art. 118/E/5
40 x 40 mm
L. 6000 mm

Art. 1275/1
40 x 4 mm
425 x 1150 mm

Art. 1373/2
60 x 16 mm
L. 3000 mm

Gratings

Art. 653/3
☐ 12 x 12 mm
⌀ 110 x 370 mm

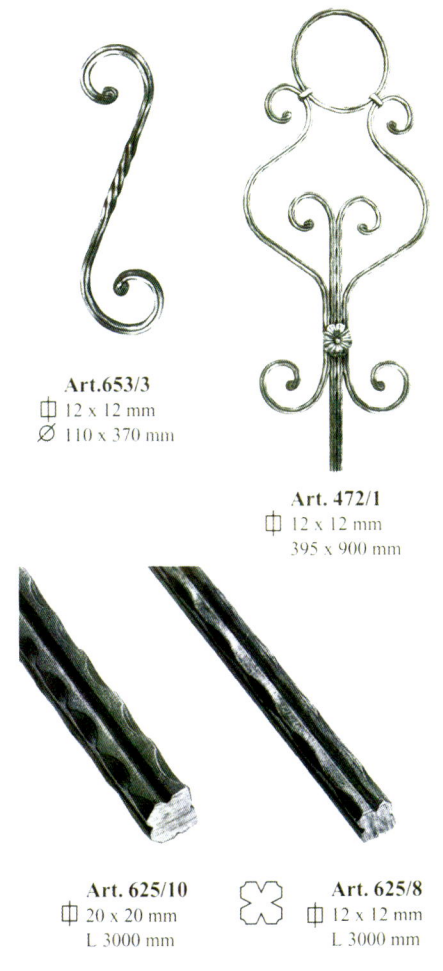

Art. 472/1
☐ 12 x 12 mm
395 x 900 mm

Art. 625/10
☐ 20 x 20 mm
L 3000 mm

Art. 625/8
☐ 12 x 12 mm
L 3000 mm

Produzione: ind.i.a. SPA

163

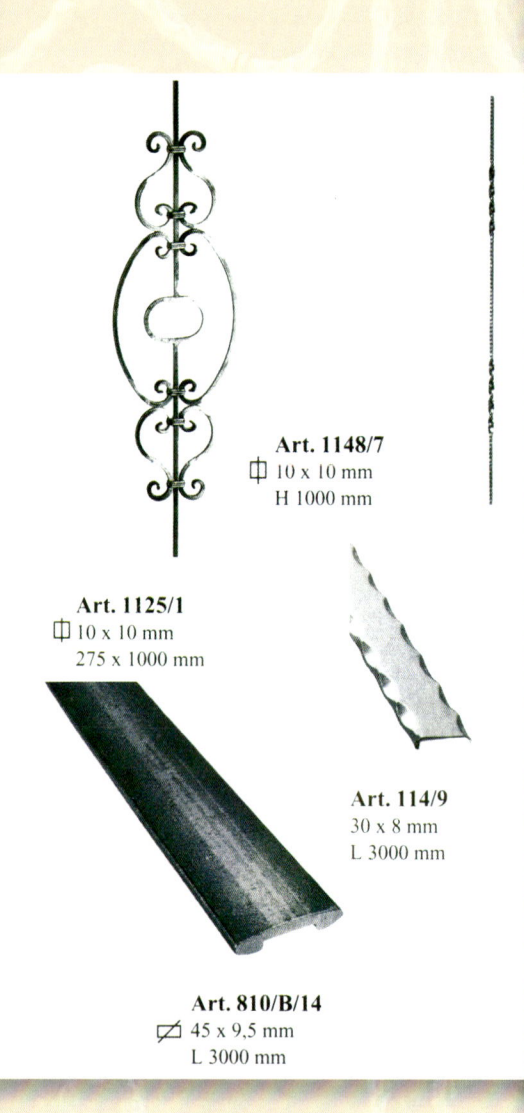

Gratings

Art. 1148/7
☐ 10 x 10 mm
H 1000 mm

Art. 1125/1
☐ 10 x 10 mm
275 x 1000 mm

Art. 114/9
30 x 8 mm
L 3000 mm

Art. 810/B/14
45 x 9,5 mm
L 3000 mm

Produzione: ind.i.a. SPA

Gratings

Art. 1368/4
⬜ 12 mm
L. 3000 mm

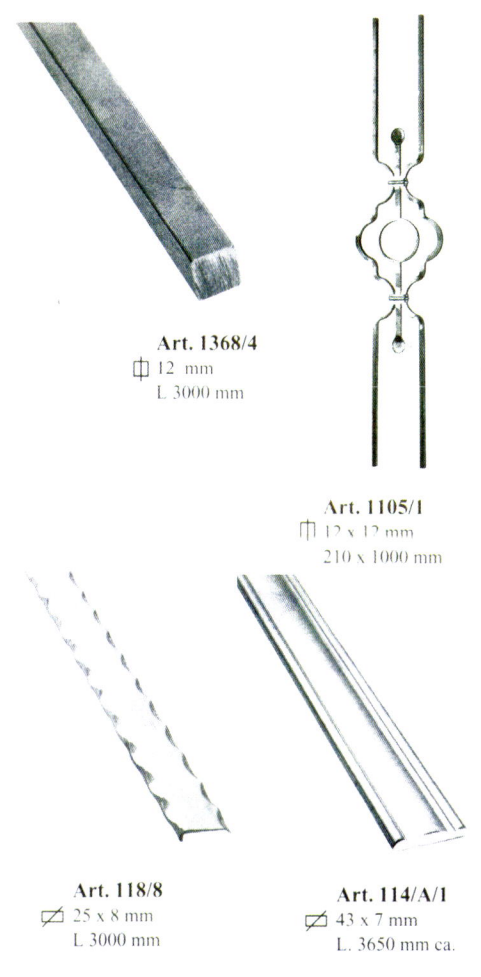

Art. 1105/1
⬜ 12 x 12 mm
210 x 1000 mm

Art. 118/8
▱ 25 x 8 mm
L. 3000 mm

Art. 114/A/1
▱ 43 x 7 mm
L. 3650 mm ca.

Produzione: ind.i.a. SPA

Gratings

Art. 158/10
⌀ 30 x 8 mm
L. 3000 mm

Art. 1368/8
⌀ 10 mm
L. 3000 mm

Art. 1073/1
⌀ 10 mm
240 x 1000 mm

Art. 158/48
⌀ 50 x 10 mm
L. 3000 mm

Produzione: ind.i.a. SPA

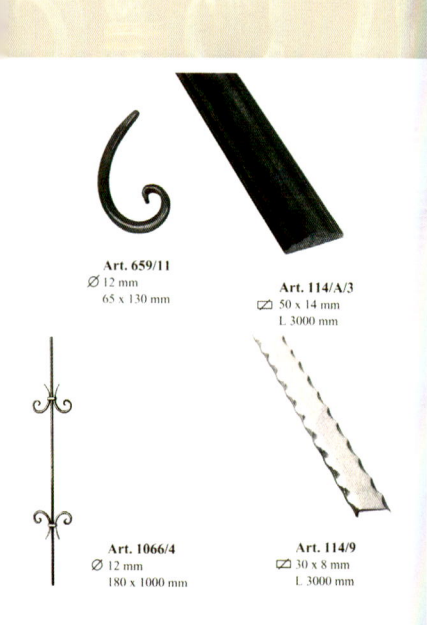

Art. 659/11
⌀ 12 mm
65 x 130 mm

Art. 114/A/3
⌀ 50 x 14 mm
L. 3000 mm

Art. 1066/4
⌀ 12 mm
180 x 1000 mm

Art. 114/9
⌀ 30 x 8 mm
L. 3000 mm

Gratings

Art. 1087/1
⌀ 12 mm
112 x 1000 mm

Art. 1087/2
⌀ 12 mm
112 x 1000 mm

Art. 114/9
▱ 30 x 8 mm
L 3000 mm

Art. 158/46
⌀ 40 x 10 mm
L 3000 mm

Produzione: ind.i.a. SPA

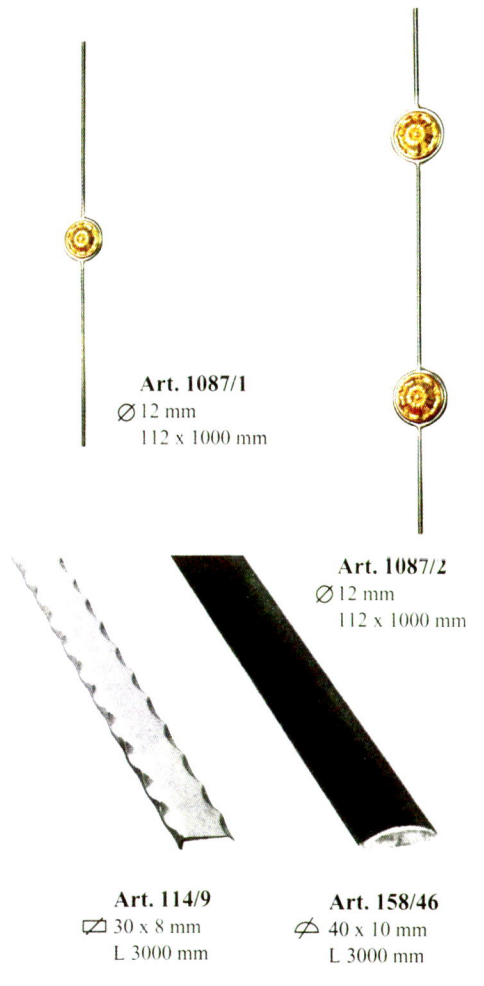

Gratings

Art. 797/2
Ø 30 mm
H 1200 mm

Art. 1404/4
Ø SFERA 55 mm
H 85 mm
Ø Base 45 mm

Art. 1071/3
Ø 12 mm
110 x 1000 mm

Art. 128/17
Ø 13 mm Foro
Ø 40 x 39 mm

Art. 128/6
Ø 12 mm Foro
Ø 40 x 65 mm

Produzione: ind.i.a. SPA

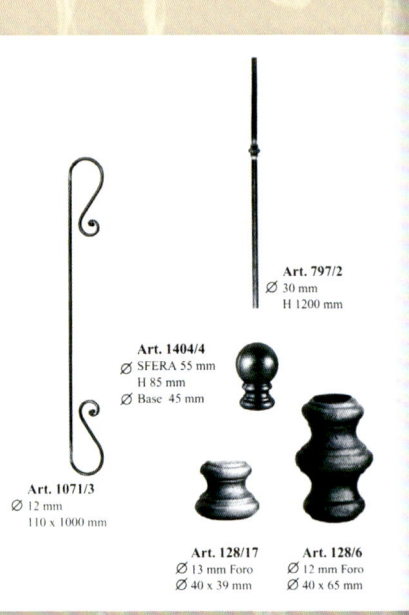

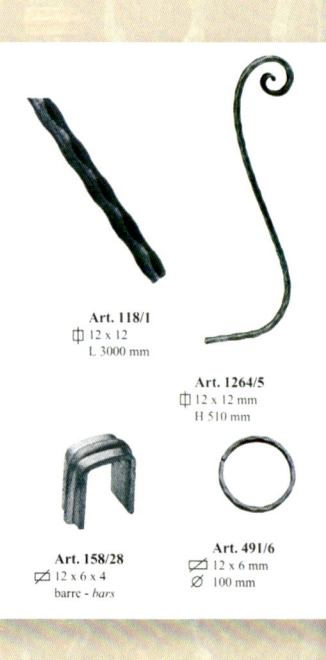

Art. 118/1
☐ 12 x 12
L 3000 mm

Art. 1264/5
☐ 12 x 12 mm
H 510 mm

Art. 158/28
12 x 6 x 4
barre - bars

Art. 491/6
12 x 6 mm
Ø 100 mm

168

Gratings

Sfere vuote Ø 45 mm

Art. 1235/1
113 x 1030 mm

Art. 114/A/3
◻ 50 x 14 mm
L 3000 mm

Art. 1231/3
Ø 30 mm
H 1000 mm

Produzione: ind.i.a. SPA

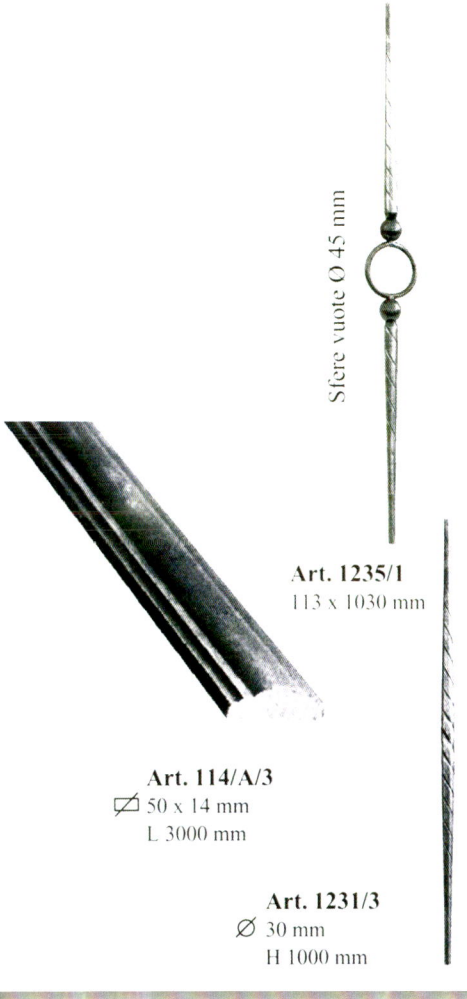

Gratings

Art. 158/10
⌀ 25 x 7 mm
L 3500 mm

Art. 114/A/3
◻ 50 x 14 mm
L 3000 mm

Art. 805/1
⌀ 30 mm
H 1200 mm

Produzione: ind.i.a. SPA

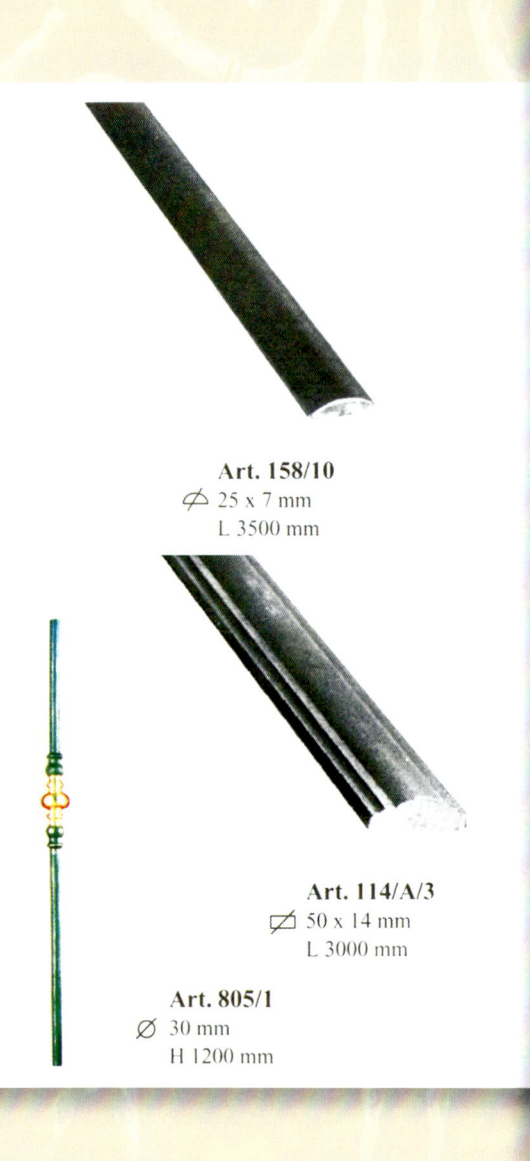

Gratings

Art. 114/9
30 x 8 mm
L 3000 mm

Art. 1231/3
⌀ 30 mm
H 1000 mm

Art. 810/B/15
55 x 10,5 mm
L 3000 mm

Produzione: ind.i.a. SPA

Gratings

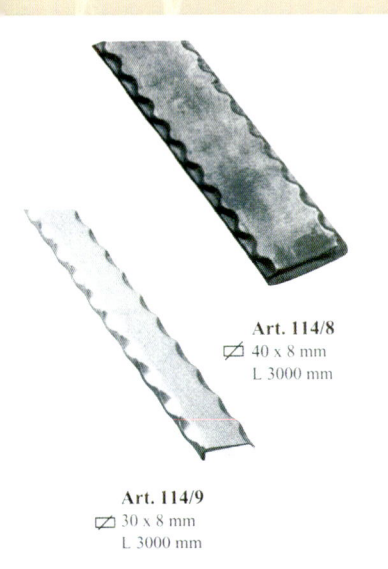

Art. 114/8
40 x 8 mm
L 3000 mm

Art. 114/9
30 x 8 mm
L 3000 mm

Produzione: ind.i.a. SPA

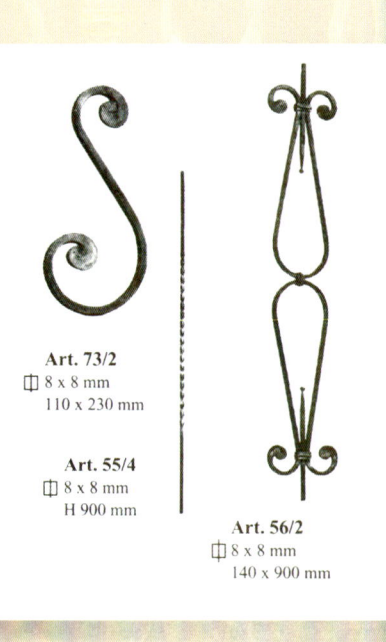

Art. 73/2
8 x 8 mm
110 x 230 mm

Art. 55/4
8 x 8 mm
H 900 mm

Art. 56/2
8 x 8 mm
140 x 900 mm

172

Gratings

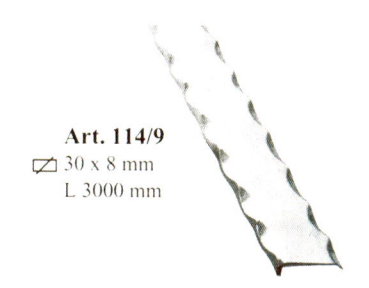

Art. 114/9
30 x 8 mm
L 3000 mm

Art. 35/2
12 x 6 mm
200 x 345 mm
SNAP-ONS

Art. 118/B/1
12 x 12 mm
H 900 mm

Produzione: ind.i.a. SPA

Gratings

Art. 118/14
◇ 40 x 8 mm
L 3000 mm

Art. 46/6
◇ 40 x 4 mm
H 800 mm
Liscio - *Plain*

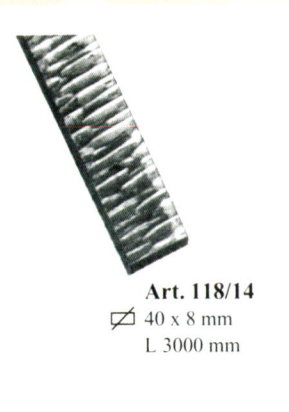

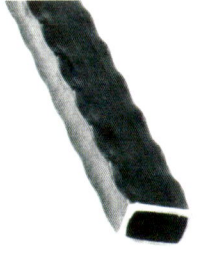

Art. 118/E/4
□ 40 x 20 mm
L 6000 mm

Produzione: ind.i.a. SPA

Gratings

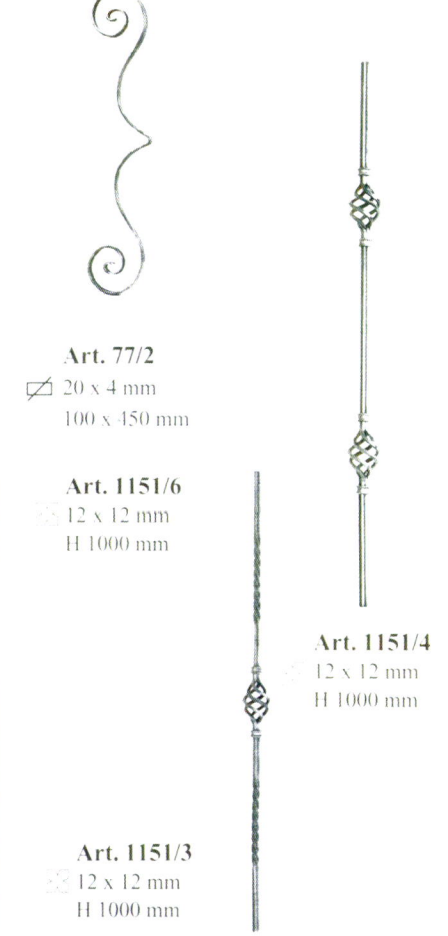

Art. 77/2
20 x 4 mm
100 x 450 mm

Art. 1151/6
12 x 12 mm
H 1000 mm

Art. 1151/4
12 x 12 mm
H 1000 mm

Art. 1151/3
12 x 12 mm
H 1000 mm

Produzione: ind.i.a. SPA

175

Gratings

Art. 36/1
◇ 12 x 6 mm
220 x 250 mm

Art. 36/2
◇ 12 x 6 mm
230 x 380 mm

Art. 1368/4
□ 12 x 12 mm
L 3000 mm

Produzione: ind.i.a. SPA

Gratings

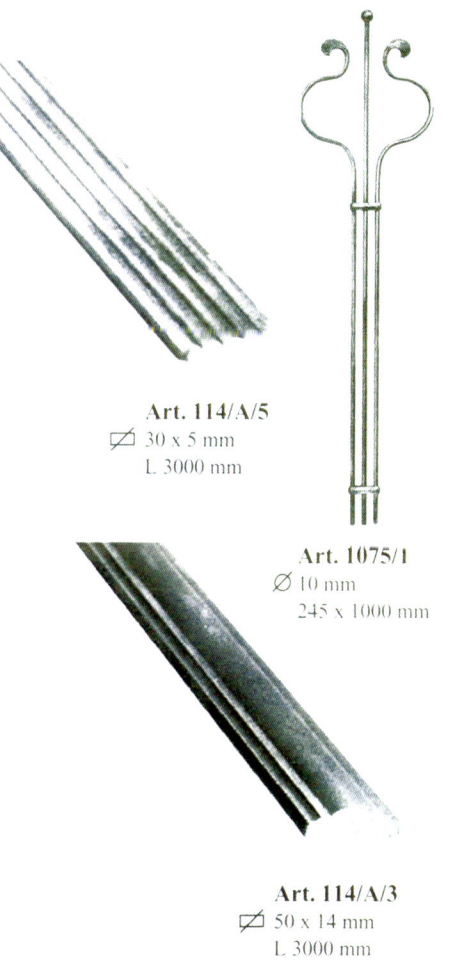

Art. 114/A/5
◇ 30 x 5 mm
L 3000 mm

Art. 1075/1
⌀ 10 mm
245 x 1000 mm

Art. 114/A/3
◇ 50 x 14 mm
L 3000 mm

Produzione: ind.i.a. SPA

Gratings

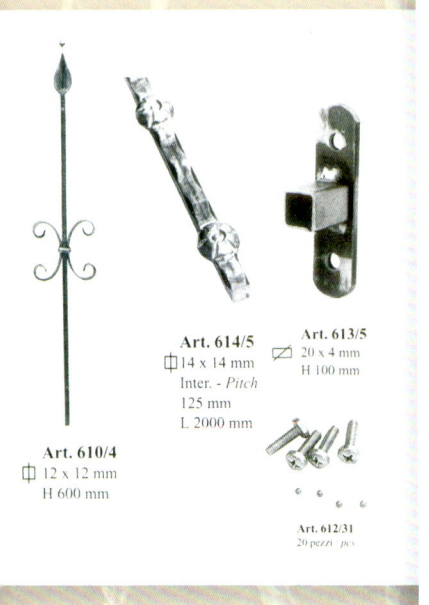

Art. 610/4
☐ 12 x 12 mm
H 600 mm

Art. 614/5
☐ 14 x 14 mm
Inter. - *Pitch*
125 mm
L. 2000 mm

Art. 613/5
20 x 4 mm
H 100 mm

Art. 612/31
20 pezzi / pcs

Produzione: ind.i.a. SPA

178

Gratings

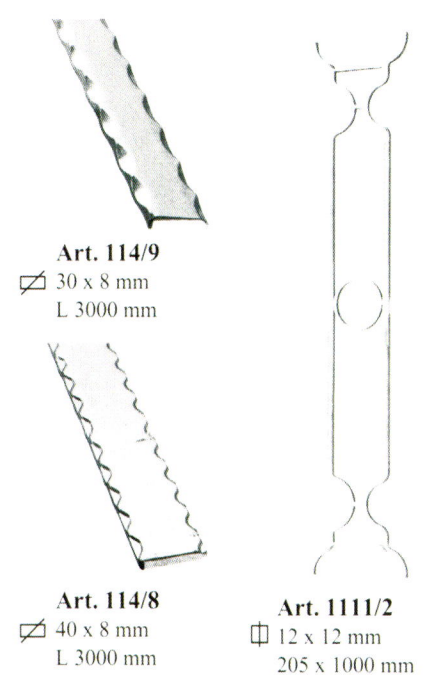

Art. 114/9
30 x 8 mm
L 3000 mm

Art. 114/8
40 x 8 mm
L 3000 mm

Art. 1111/2
12 x 12 mm
205 x 1000 mm

Produzione: ind.i.a. SPA

Gratings

Art. 1207/1
◻ 60 mm Tubo - *Tube*
85 x 1200 mm

Art. 810/A/19
38 x 25 mm
L 3000 mm

Art. 810/A/21
60,5 x 19 mm
L 3000 mm

Art. 1167/4
Ø 12 mm
H 1000 mm

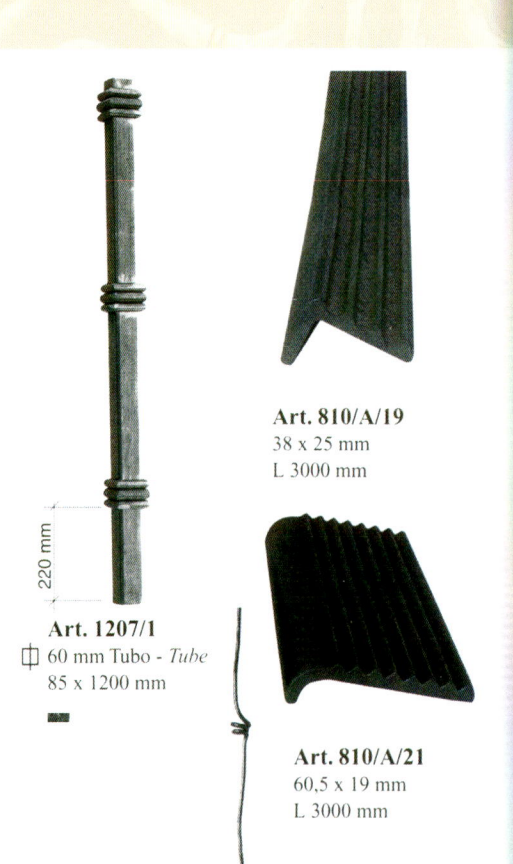

Produzione: ind.i.a. SPA

Gratings

Art. 1084/1
□ 12 mm
175 x 1000 mm

Art. 1120/1
▱ 12 x 6 mm
270 x 1000 mm

Art. 810/B/8
▱ 55 x 17 mm
L 6000 mm

Produzione: ind.i.a. SPA

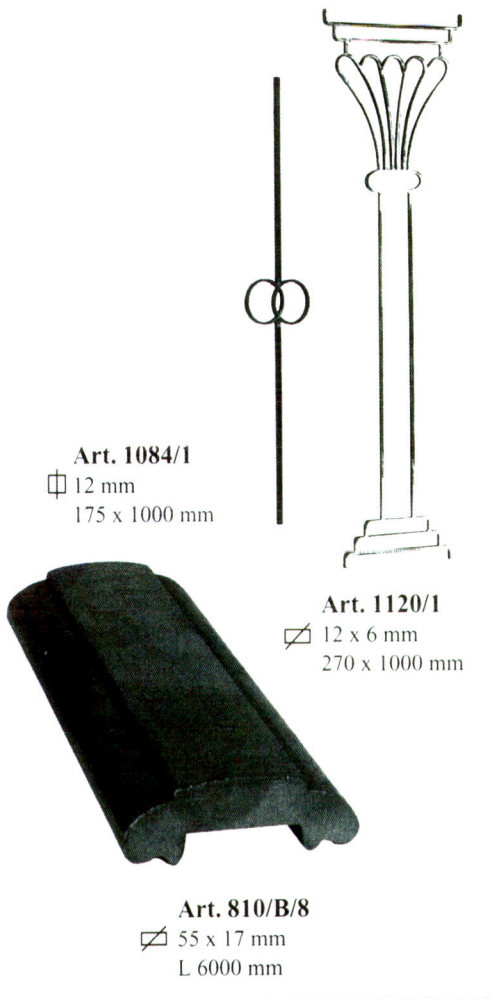

Gratings

Art. 1175/4
12 x 12 mm
40 x 1000 mm

Art. 1175/3
12 x 12 mm
40 x 1000 mm

Art. 114/9
30 x 8 mm
L 3000 mm

Produzione: ind.i.a. SPA

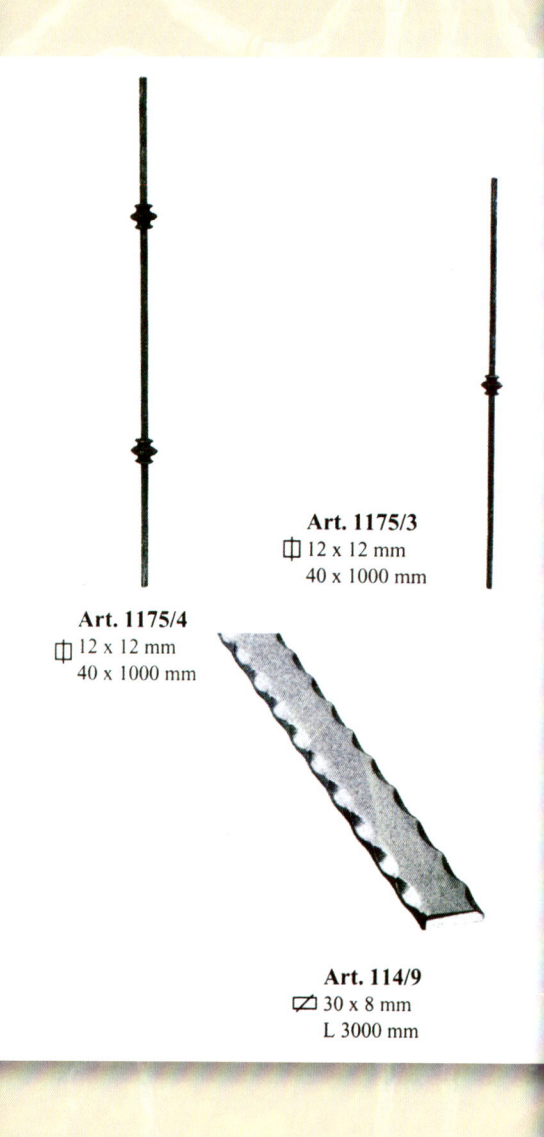

Gratings

Art. 80/A/1
12 x 6 mm
110 x 270 mm

Art. 543/3
14 x 8 mm
120 x 500 mm

Art. 116/A/4
3 mm
Ø 65 mm

Art. 499/1
Ø 12 mm
H 900 mm

Art. 114/9
30 x 8 mm
L 3000 mm

Art. 114/5
40 x 8 mm
L 3000 mm

Produzione: ind.i.a. SPA

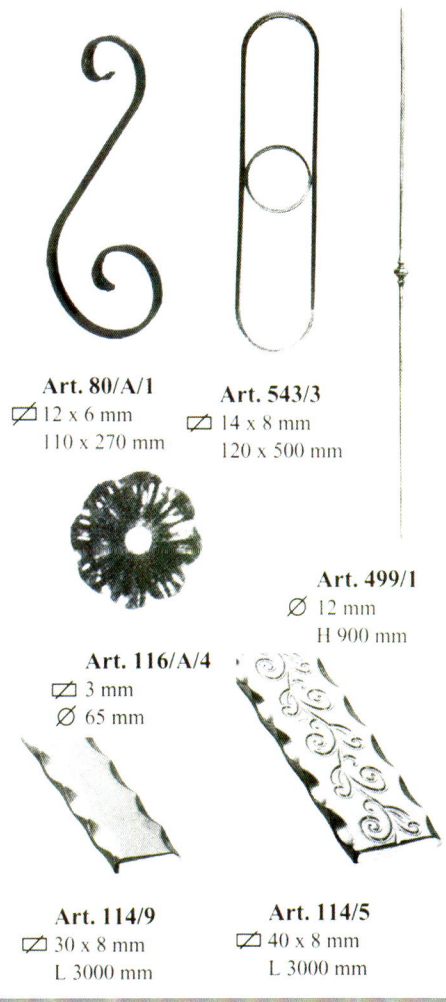

Gratings

Art. 114/A/2
◊ 53 x 9 mm
L 3650 mm

Art. 1097/3
▢ 12 x 12 mm
105 x 1000 mm

Art. 1368/4
▢ 12 x 12 mm
L 3000 mm

Produzione: ind.i.a. SPA

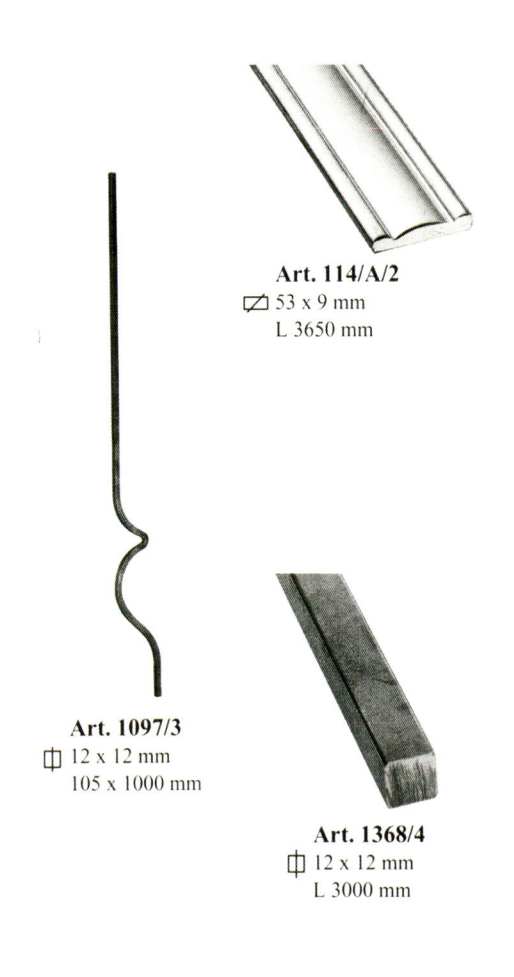

Gratings

Art. 1101/1
20 x 8 mm
240 x 1000 mm

Art. 1368/16
20 x 6 mm
L 3000 mm

Art. 114/A/3
50 x 14 mm
L 3000 mm

Produzione: ind.i.a. SPA

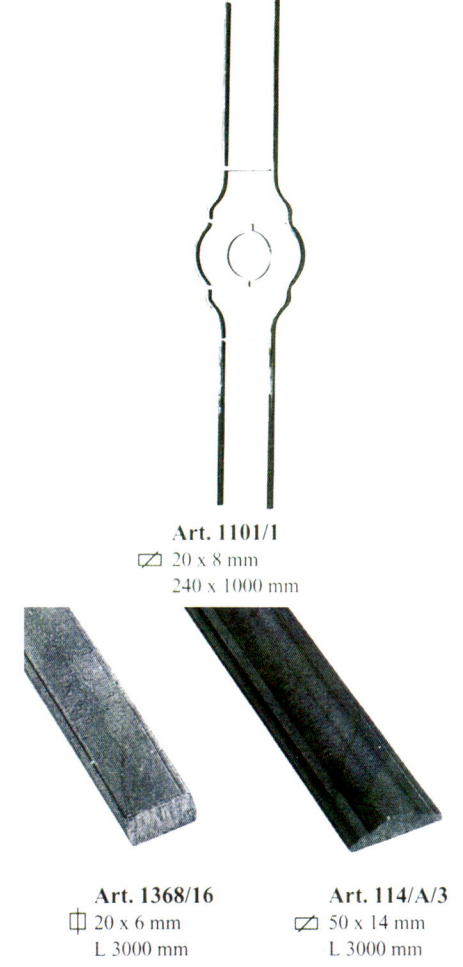

Gratings

Art. 1085/1
⌀ 12 mm
112 x 1000 mm

Art. 1085/2
⌀ 12 mm
112 x 1000 mm

Art. 114/9
◻ 30 x 8 mm
L 3000 mm

Produzione: ind.i.a. SPA

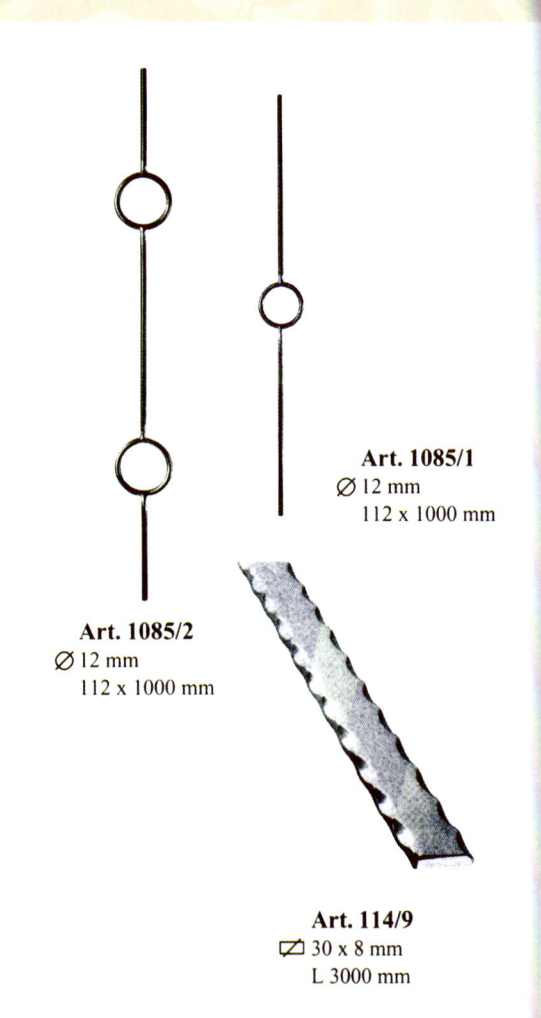

186

Gratings

Art. 85/9
Fascetta L. 37 mm
Collar 37 mm

Art. 1089/4
☐ 12 x 12 mm
165 x 1000 mm

Art. 1368/4
☐ 12 x 12 mm
L 3000 mm

Art. 114/A/3
▱ 50 x 14 mm
L 3000 mm

Produzione: ind.i.a. SPA

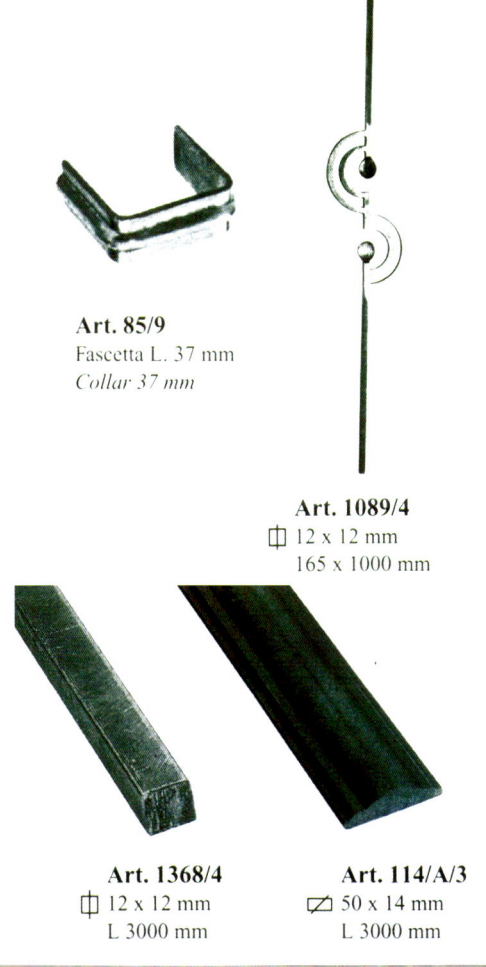

Gratings

Art. 1086/1
12 mm
112 x 1000 mm

Art. 1086/2
12 mm
112 x 1000 mm

Art. 810/B/2
◱ 40 x 10,5 mm
L 3000 mm

Art. 114/9
◱ 30 x 8 mm
L 3000 mm

Produzione: ind.i.a. SPA

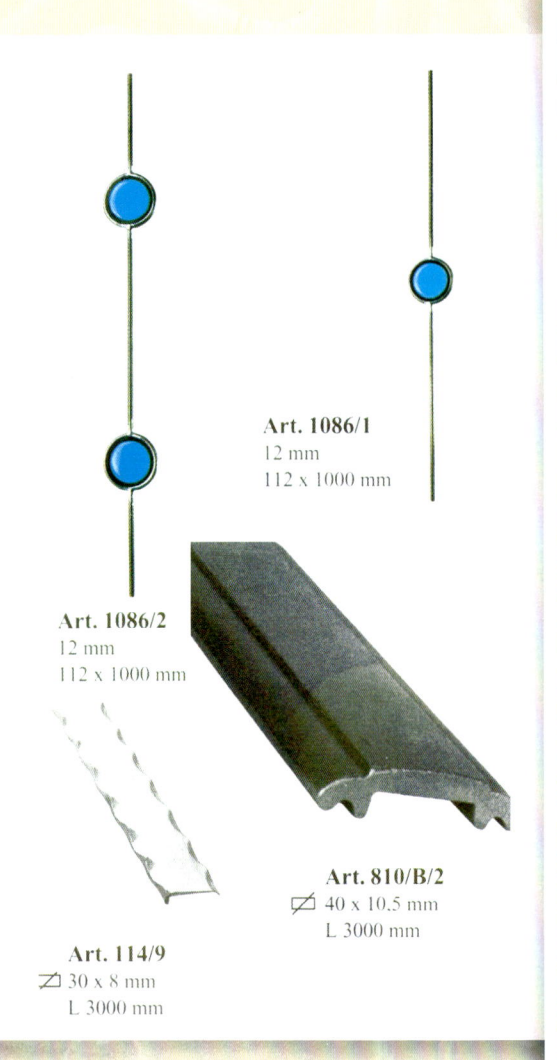

Gratings

Art. 1368/16
⬜ 20 x 6 mm
L 3000 mm

Art. 1101/1
⬜ 20 x 8 mm
240 x 1000 mm

Art. 810/5
⌀ 40 x 20 mm
L 3000 mm

Produzione: ind.i.a. SPA

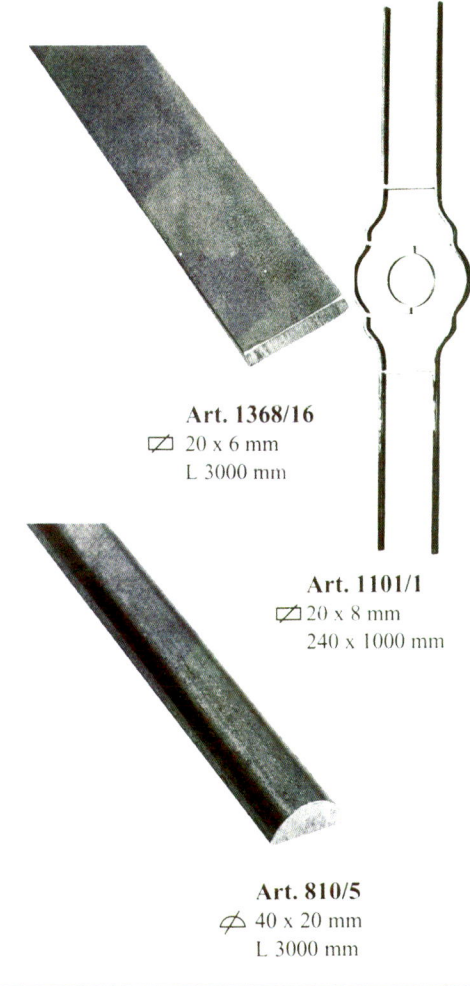

Gratings

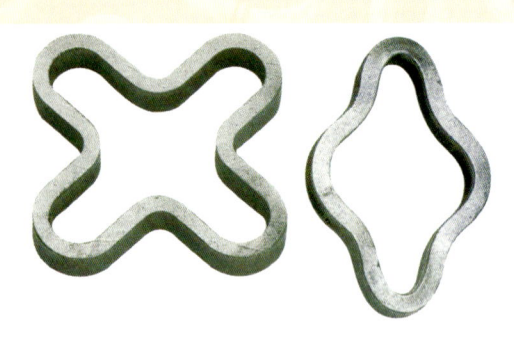

Art. 1323/9
◰ 12 x 6 mm
⌀ 100 mm
L 80 mm

Art. 1323/7
◰ 12 x 6 mm
100 x 170 mm

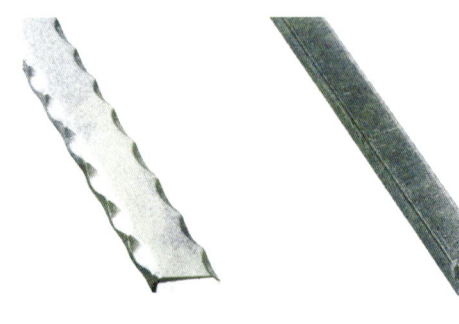

Art. 118/8
◰ 25 x 8 mm
L 3000 mm

Art. 1368/4
⬜ 12 x 12 mm
L 3000 mm

Produzione: ind.i.a. SPA

Gratings

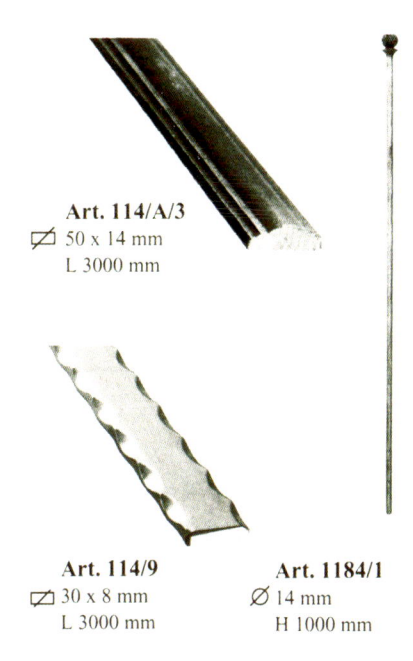

Art. 114/A/3
50 x 14 mm
L 3000 mm

Art. 114/9
30 x 8 mm
L 3000 mm

Art. 1184/1
Ø 14 mm
H 1000 mm

Produzione: ind.i.a. SPA

Gratings

Art. 1067/2
⌀ 12 mm
H 1000 mm

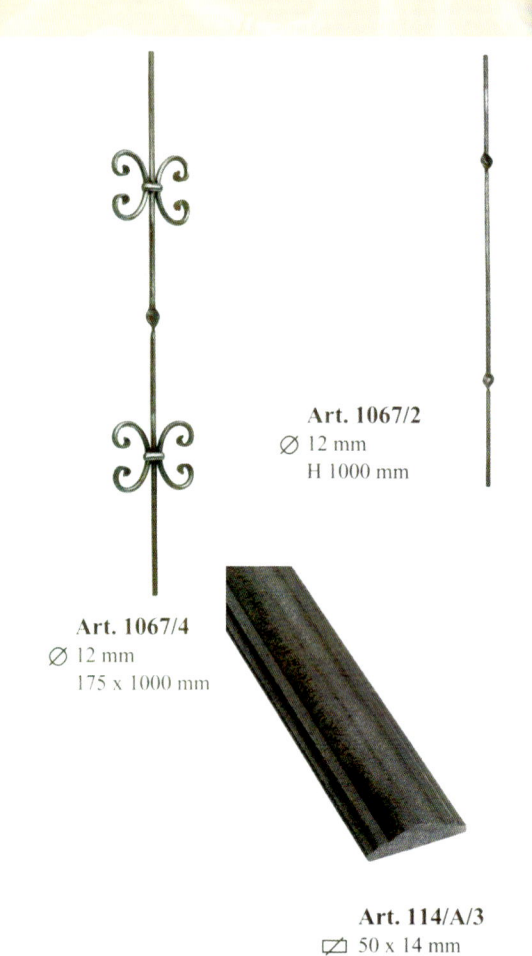

Art. 1067/4
⌀ 12 mm
175 x 1000 mm

Art. 114/A/3
◻ 50 x 14 mm
L 3000 mm

Produzione: ind.i.a. SPA

Gratings

Art. 491/8
⊡ 12 mm
⌀ 100 mm
Liscio - *Plain*

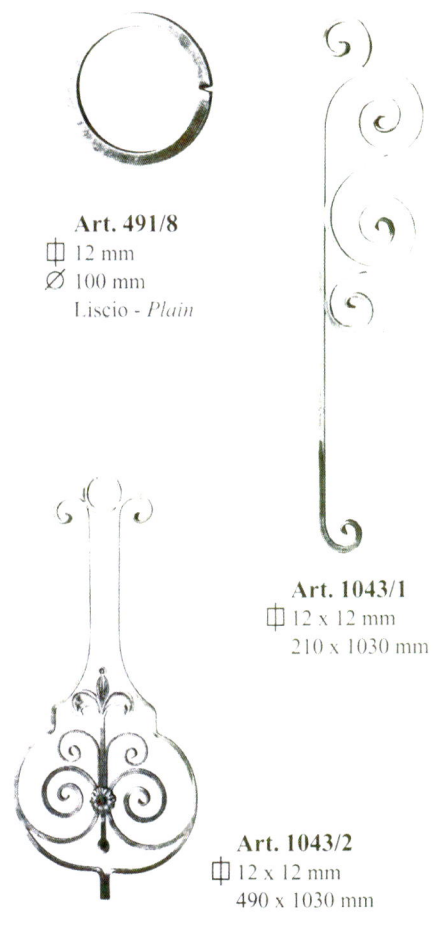

Art. 1043/1
⊡ 12 x 12 mm
210 x 1030 mm

Art. 1043/2
⊡ 12 x 12 mm
490 x 1030 mm

Produzione: ind.i.a. SPA

Gratings

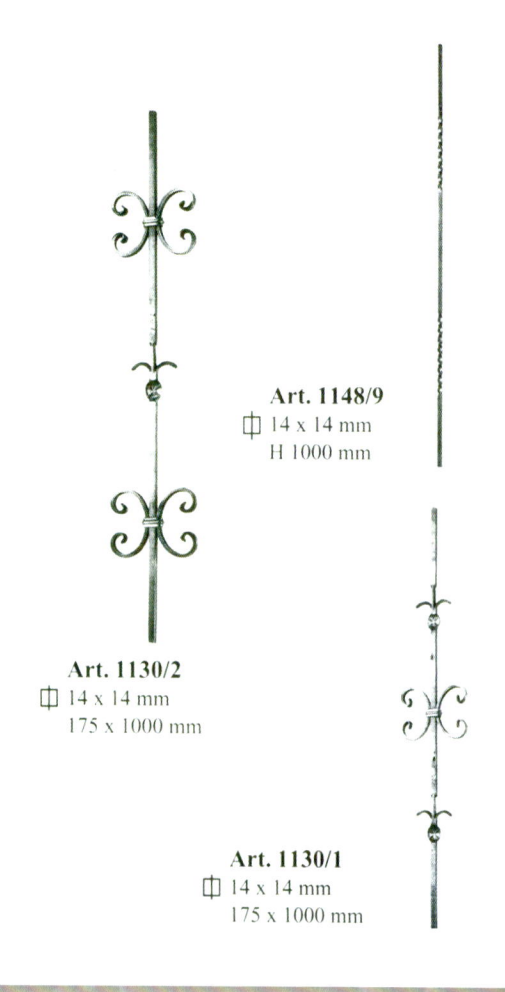

Art. 1148/9
▫ 14 x 14 mm
H 1000 mm

Art. 1130/2
▫ 14 x 14 mm
175 x 1000 mm

Art. 1130/1
▫ 14 x 14 mm
175 x 1000 mm

Produzione: ind.i.a. SPA

194

Gratings

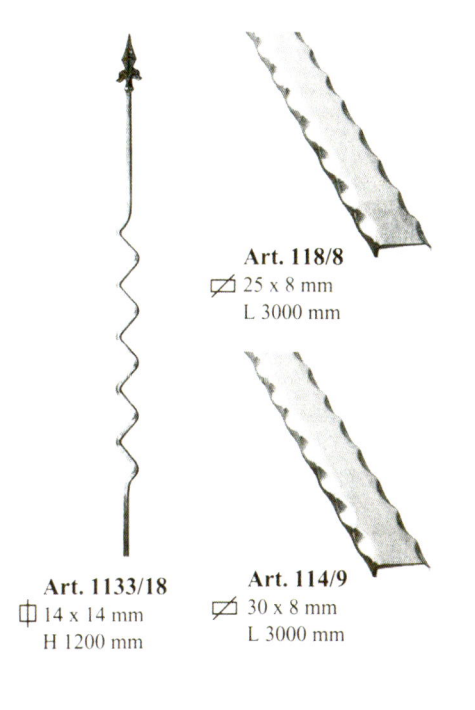

Art. 1133/18
◻ 14 x 14 mm
H 1200 mm

Art. 118/8
▱ 25 x 8 mm
L 3000 mm

Art. 114/9
▱ 30 x 8 mm
L 3000 mm

Produzione: ind.i.a. SPA

Gratings

Art. 120/1
⌀ 40 mm sfera - *boss*
H 220 mm

Art. 88/P/3
▱ 14 x 8 mm
80 x 130 mm

Art. 120/3
⌀ 30 mm sfera - *boss*
H 170 mm

Art. 128/15
⌀ 50 x 78 mm
⌀ 22 mm Foro - *Hole*

Art. 181/7
▱ 18 x 5 mm
Fascetta - *Collar*

Art. 697/5
⌀ 16 mm
⌀ 8 mm Foro

Produzione: ind.i.a. SPA

Gratings

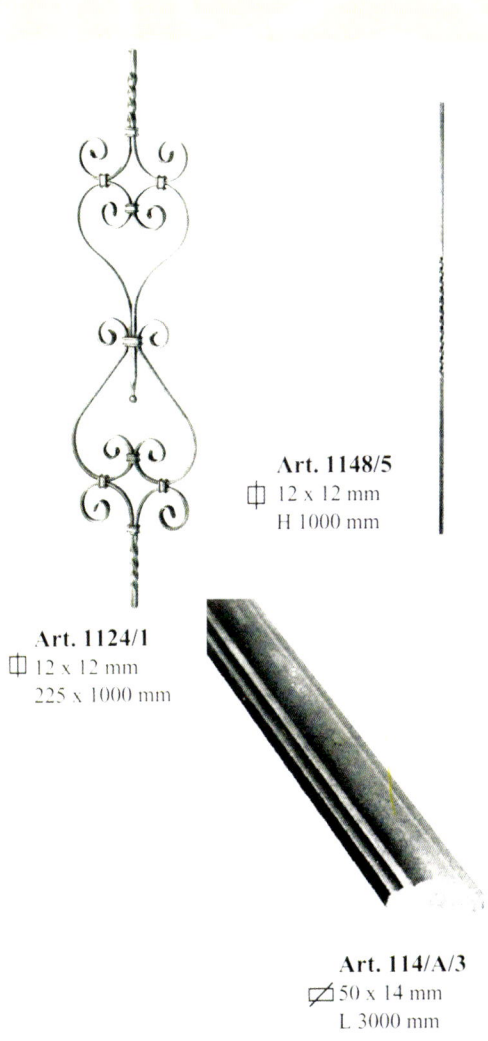

Art. 1148/5
☐ 12 x 12 mm
H 1000 mm

Art. 1124/1
☐ 12 x 12 mm
225 x 1000 mm

Art. 114/A/3
◇ 50 x 14 mm
L 3000 mm

Produzione: ind.i.a. SPA

Gratings

Art. 42/2
Ø 16 mm
13 Fori - *Holes*
Int. - *Pitch* 150 mm
L 2000 mm

Art. 727/11
Ø 30 mm
35 x 120 mm

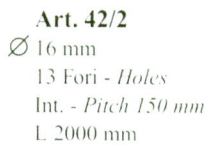

Art. 739/3
Ø 45 x 54 mm
Ø 16 mm foro - *hole*

Produzione: ind.i.a. SPA

Gratings

Art. 94/P/9
12 x 12 mm
Liscio - *Plain*

Art. 85/8
12 x 12 x 3 barre
Fascetta L=25 mm
Collar 25 mm

Art. 1046/2
12 x 12 mm
200 x 900 mm

Art. 94/Q/5
12 x 12 mm
Liscio - *Plain*

Produzione: ind.i.a. SPA

Gratings

Art. 1394/25
⌀ 25 mm
⌀ 12,5 mm Foro - *Hole*
2 mm Spessore - *Thickness*

Art. 1208/3
⌀ 12 mm
H 1000 mm

Art. 1067/2
⌀ 12 mm
H 1000 mm

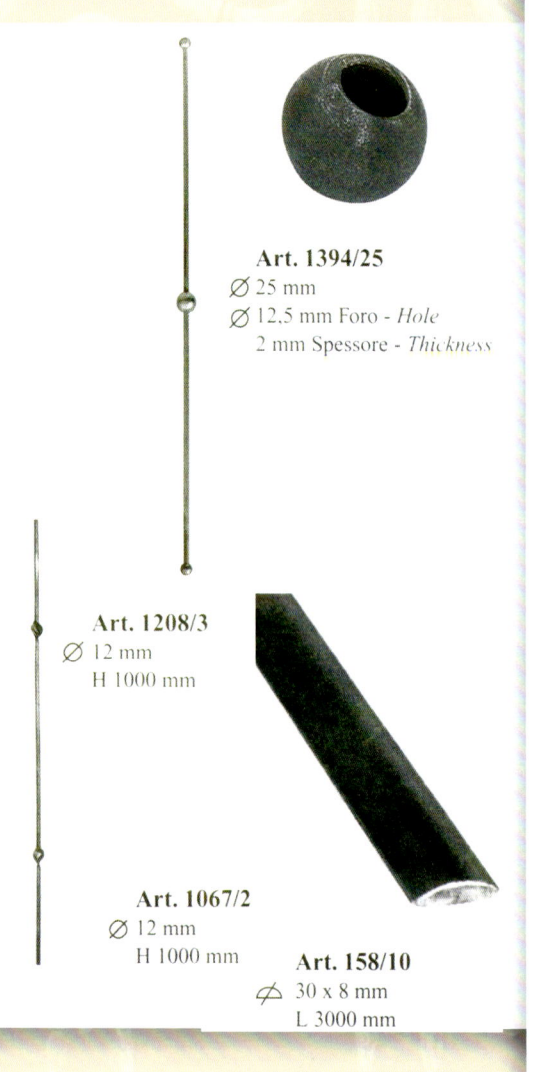

Art. 158/10
⌀ 30 x 8 mm
L 3000 mm

Produzione: ind.i.a. SPA

200

Gratings

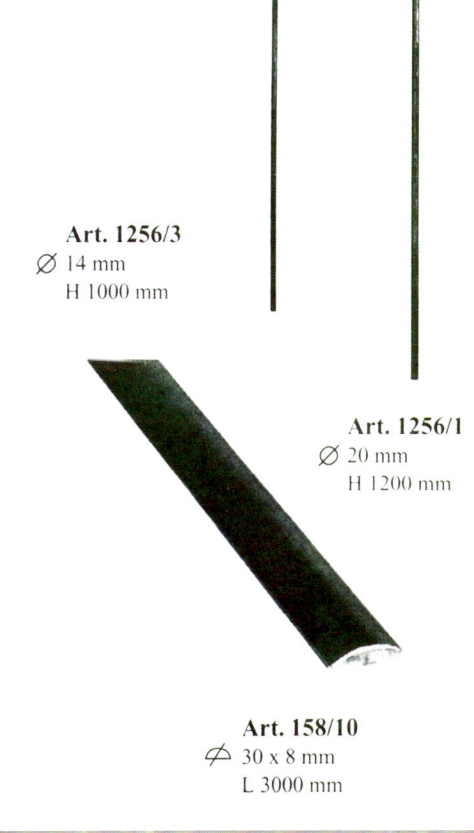

Art. 1256/3
⌀ 14 mm
H 1000 mm

Art. 1256/1
⌀ 20 mm
H 1200 mm

Art. 158/10
⌀ 30 x 8 mm
L 3000 mm

Produzione: ind.i.a. SPA

201

Gratings

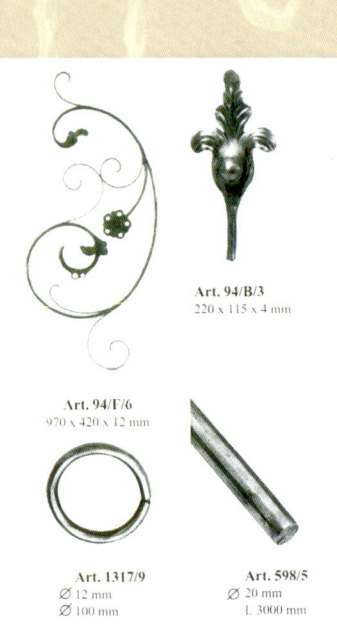

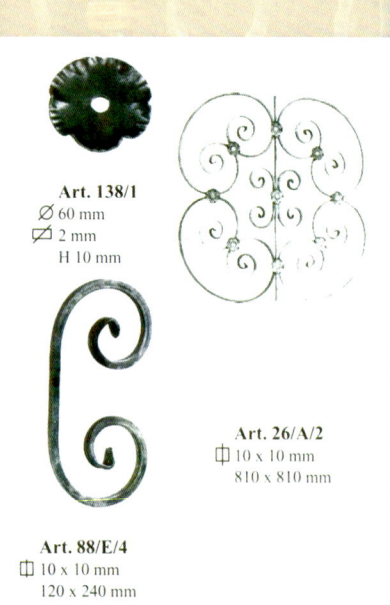

Art. 94/B/3
220 x 115 x 4 mm

Art. 94/F/6
970 x 420 x 12 mm

Art. 1317/9
Ø 12 mm
Ø 100 mm

Art. 598/5
Ø 20 mm
L 3000 mm

Produzione: ind.i.a. SPA

Art. 138/1
Ø 60 mm
☐ 2 mm
H 10 mm

Art. 26/A/2
☐ 10 x 10 mm
810 x 810 mm

Art. 88/E/4
☐ 10 x 10 mm
120 x 240 mm

Gratings

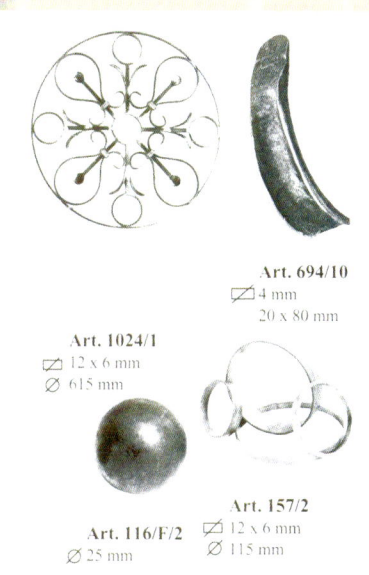

Art. 694/10
□ 4 mm
20 x 80 mm

Art. 1024/1
□ 12 x 6 mm
Ø 615 mm

Art. 116/F/2
Ø 25 mm

Art. 157/2
□ 12 x 6 mm
Ø 115 mm

Produzione: ind.i.a. SPA

Art. 739/2
Ø 14 mm
Foro - *Hole*

Art. 727/10
Ø 55 mm
40 x 150 mm

Art. 42/1
Ø 14 mm - L 2000 mm
14 n. Fori - *Holes*
140 mm Inter. - *Pitch*

Gratings

Art. 118/7
◇ 20 x 8 mm
L 3000 mm

Art. 132/A/3
□ 12 x 12 mm
H 1500 mm

Art. 81/7
□ 8 x 8 mm
73 x 122 mm

Produzione: ind.i.a. SPA

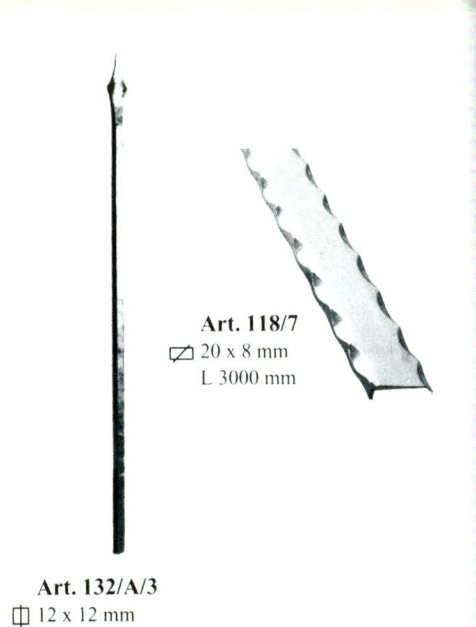

Gratings

Art. 112/6
◻ 30 mm
H 1200 mm

Art. 75/14
◇ 25 x 4 mm
270 x 720 mm
Martellato - *Hammered*

Art. 120/2
Ø 35 mm sfera - *boss*
H 200 mm

Art. 117/3
Ø 25 mm

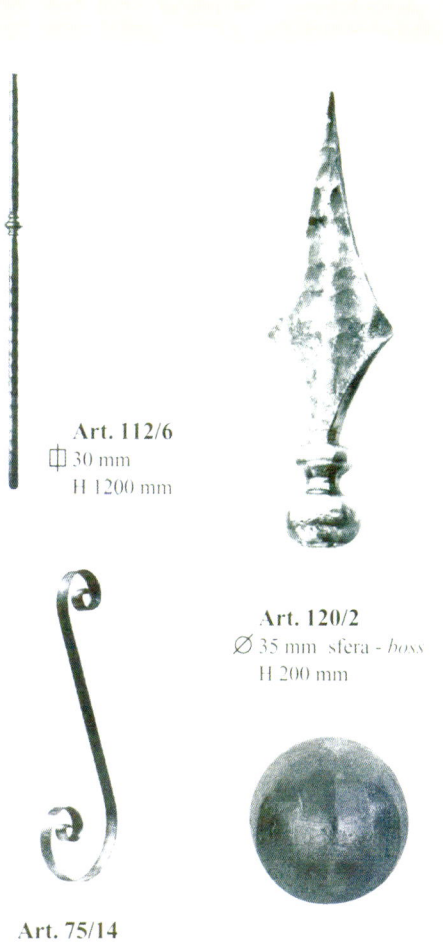

Produzione: ind.i.a. SPA

Gratings

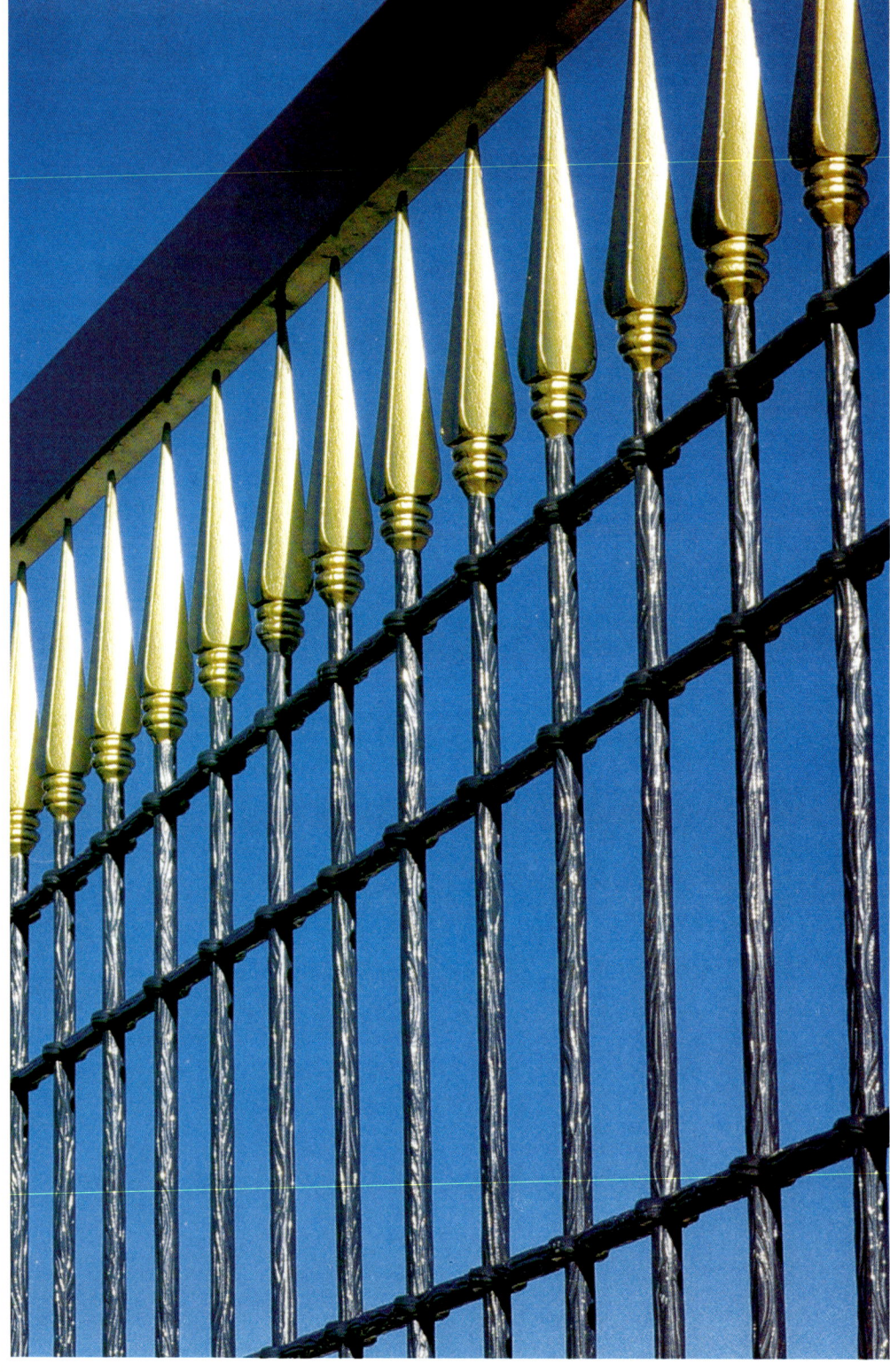

Art. 724/1
Ø 35 mm
H 295 mm

Art. 606/4
Ø 20 mm - L 2000 mm
170 mm Inter. - *Pitch*
11 Fori per barra - *Holes per bar*

Art. 599/7
Ø 20 mm
L 3000 mm

Produzione: ind.i.a. SPA

Gratings

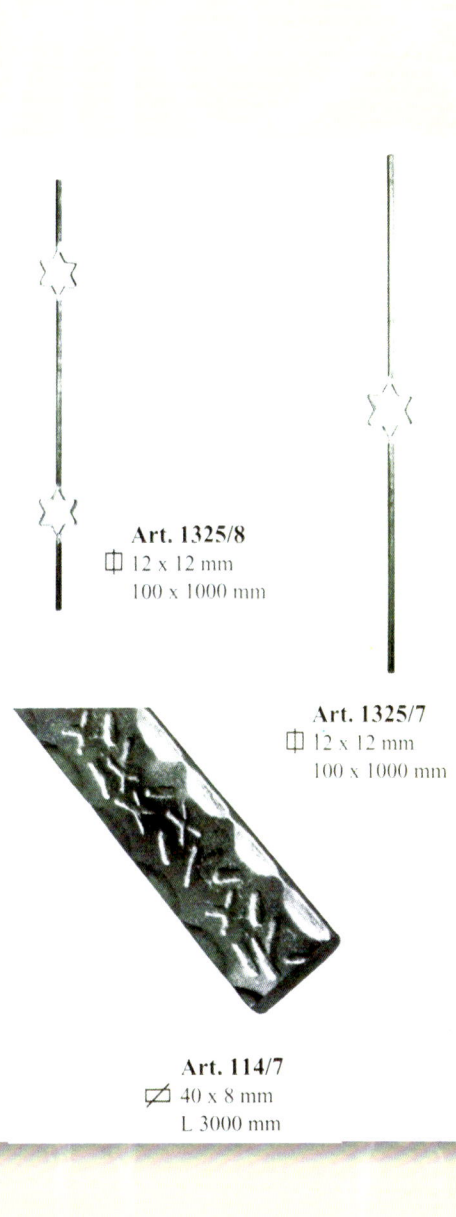

Art. 1325/8
⊡ 12 x 12 mm
100 x 1000 mm

Art. 1325/7
⊡ 12 x 12 mm
100 x 1000 mm

Art. 114/7
⊡ 40 x 8 mm
L 3000 mm

Produzione: ind.i.a. SPA

Gratings

Art. 1021/1
▢ 12 x 6 mm
Ø 590 mm

Art. 116/F/3
Ø 30 mm

Art. 1299/2
▢ 12 x 6 mm
140 x 140 mm

Art. 157/1
▢ 12 x 6 mm

Produzione: ind.i.a. SPA

Gratings

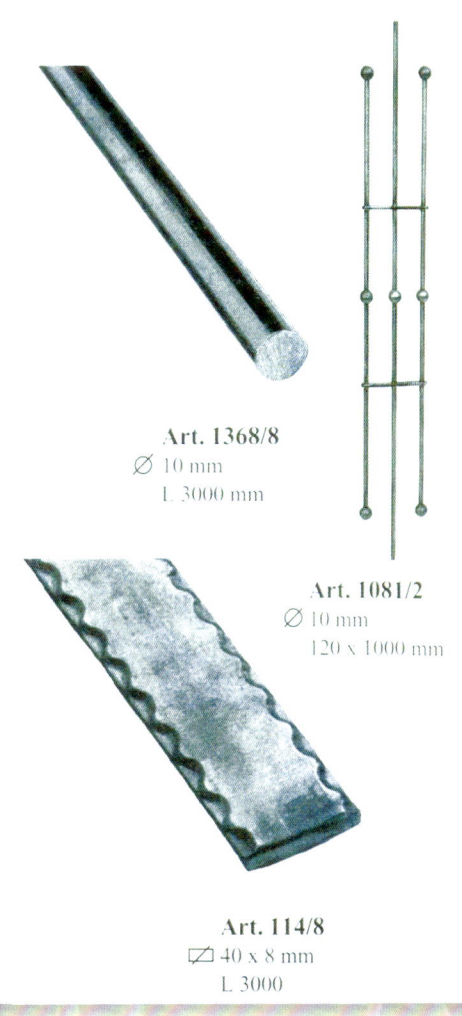

Art. 1368/8
Ø 10 mm
L. 3000 mm

Art. 1081/2
Ø 10 mm
120 x 1000 mm

Art. 114/8
◻ 40 x 8 mm
L. 3000

Produzione: ind.i.a. SPA

Gratings

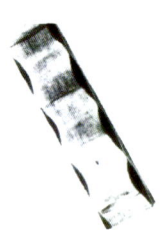

Art. 118/A/6
30 x 8 mm
L 3000 mm

Art. 1185/1
12 x 12 mm
H 1000 mm

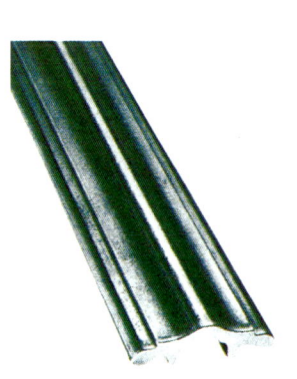

Art. 80/A/3
12 x 6 mm

Art. 810/B/22
44,5 x 14,5 mm
L 6000 mm

Produzione: ind.i.a. SPA

Gratings

Art. 134/2
⬜ 12 x 12 mm
H 1000 mm

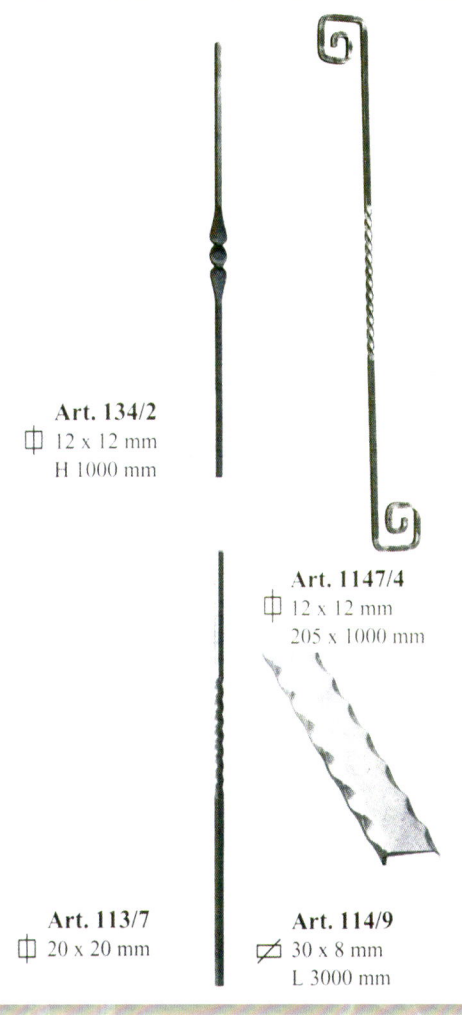

Art. 1147/4
⬜ 12 x 12 mm
205 x 1000 mm

Art. 113/7
⬜ 20 x 20 mm

Art. 114/9
▱ 30 x 8 mm
L 3000 mm

Produzione: ind.i.a. SPA

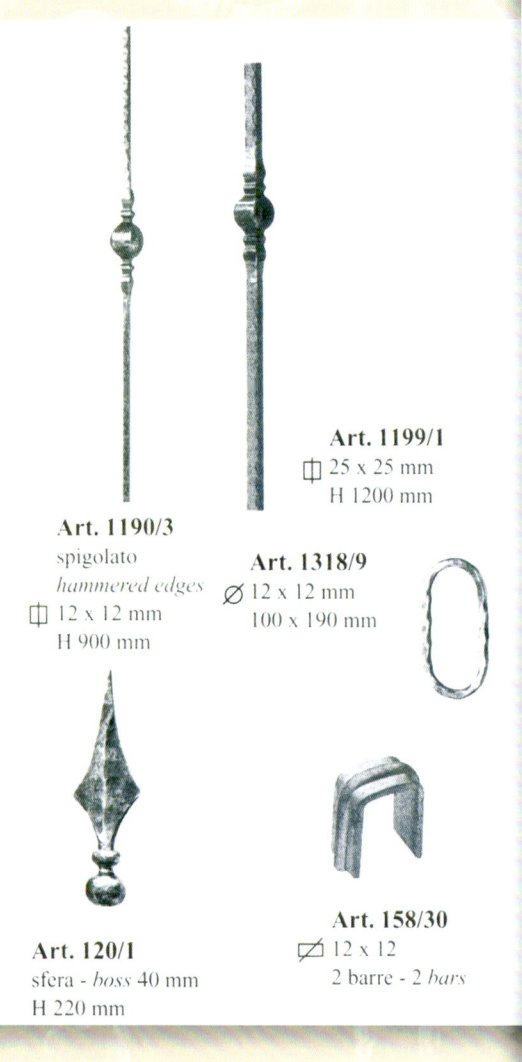

Gratings

Art. 1190/3
spigolato
hammered edges
☐ 12 x 12 mm
H 900 mm

Art. 1199/1
☐ 25 x 25 mm
H 1200 mm

Art. 1318/9
Ø 12 x 12 mm
100 x 190 mm

Art. 120/1
sfera - *boss* 40 mm
H 220 mm

Art. 158/30
☐ 12 x 12
2 barre - *2 bars*

Produzione: ind.i.a. SPA

212

Gratings

Art. 1258/6
⌀ 14 mm
H 1000 mm

Art. 1205/1
⌀ 25 mm
H 1200 mm

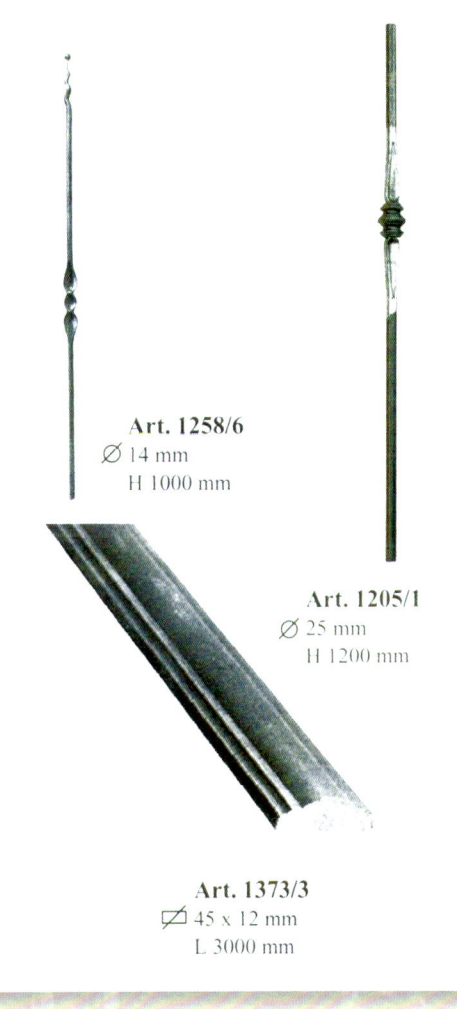

Art. 1373/3
▱ 45 x 12 mm
L 3000 mm

Produzione: ind.i.a. SPA

213

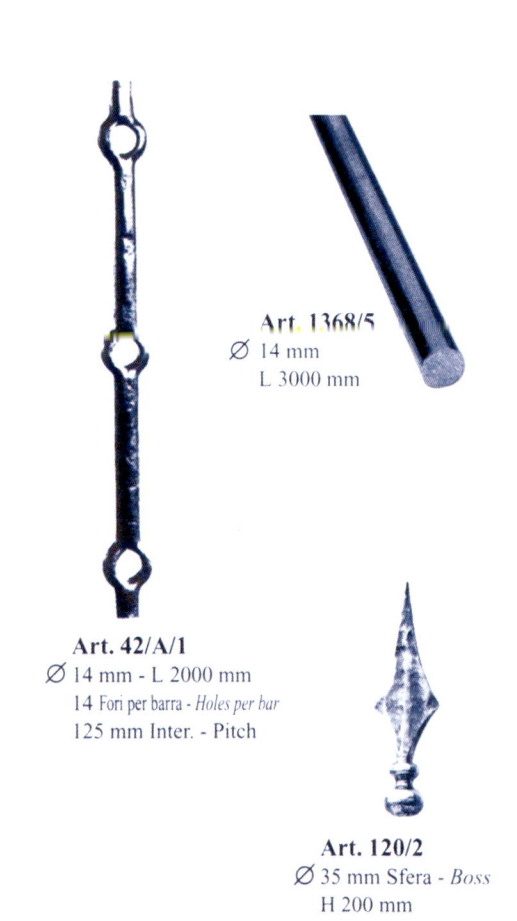

Gratings

Art. 1368/5
⌀ 14 mm
L 3000 mm

Art. 42/A/1
⌀ 14 mm - L 2000 mm
14 Fori per barra - *Holes per bar*
125 mm Inter. - *Pitch*

Art. 120/2
⌀ 35 mm Sfera - *Boss*
H 200 mm

Produzione: ind.i.a. SPA

Gratings

Art. 53/3
⊡ 12 x 12 mm
H 900 mm

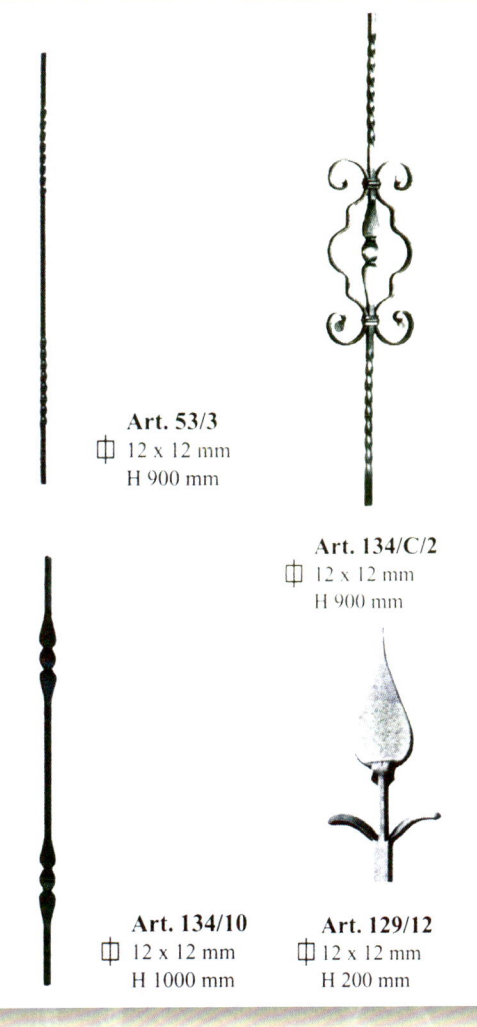

Art. 134/C/2
⊡ 12 x 12 mm
H 900 mm

Art. 134/10
⊡ 12 x 12 mm
H 1000 mm

Art. 129/12
⊡ 12 x 12 mm
H 200 mm

Produzione: ind.i.a. SPA

Gratings

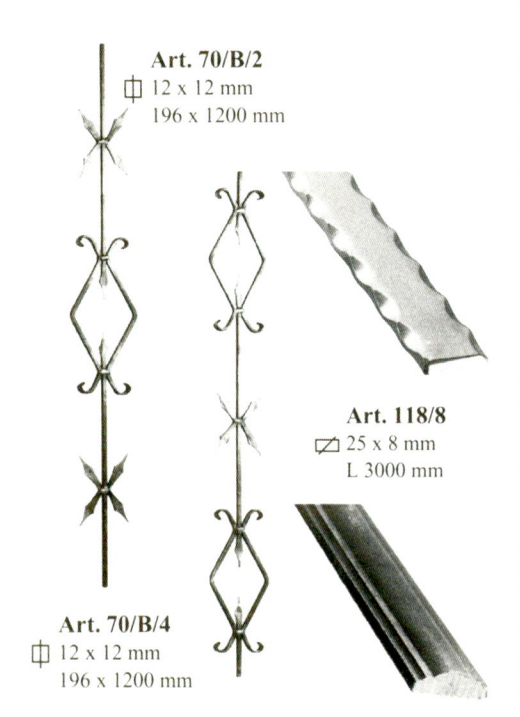

Art. 70/B/2
□ 12 x 12 mm
196 x 1200 mm

Art. 118/8
◇ 25 x 8 mm
L 3000 mm

Art. 70/B/4
□ 12 x 12 mm
196 x 1200 mm

Art. 1373/4
◇ 40 x 11 mm
L 3000 mm

Produzione: ind.i.a. SPA

Gratings

Gratings

Art. 132/A/11
□ 14 x 14 mm
H 1200 mm

Art. 132/A/22
□ 14 x 14 mm
H 900 mm

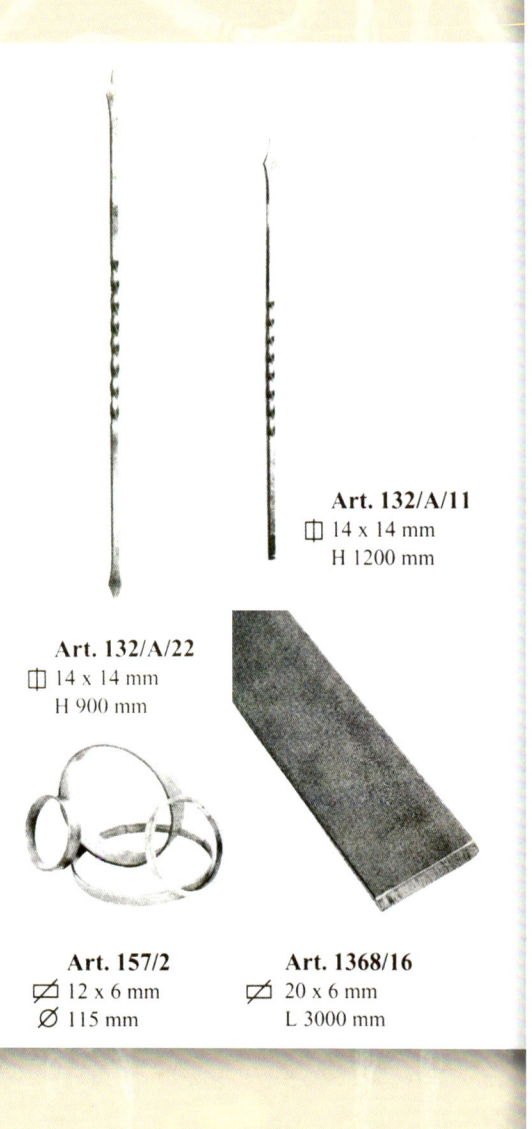

Art. 157/2
◇ 12 x 6 mm
Ø 115 mm

Art. 1368/16
◇ 20 x 6 mm
L 3000 mm

Produzione: ind.i.a. SPA

Gratings

Art. 717/5
50 x 285 mm
▱ 3 mm

Art. 540/2
⌀ 12 mm
250 x 720 mm

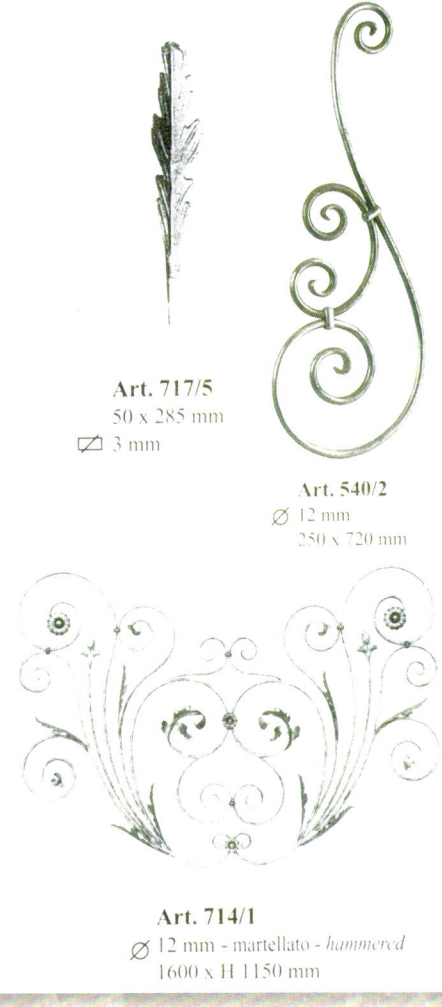

Art. 714/1
⌀ 12 mm - *martellato* - *hammered*
1600 x H 1150 mm

Produzione: ind.i.a. SPA

Gratings

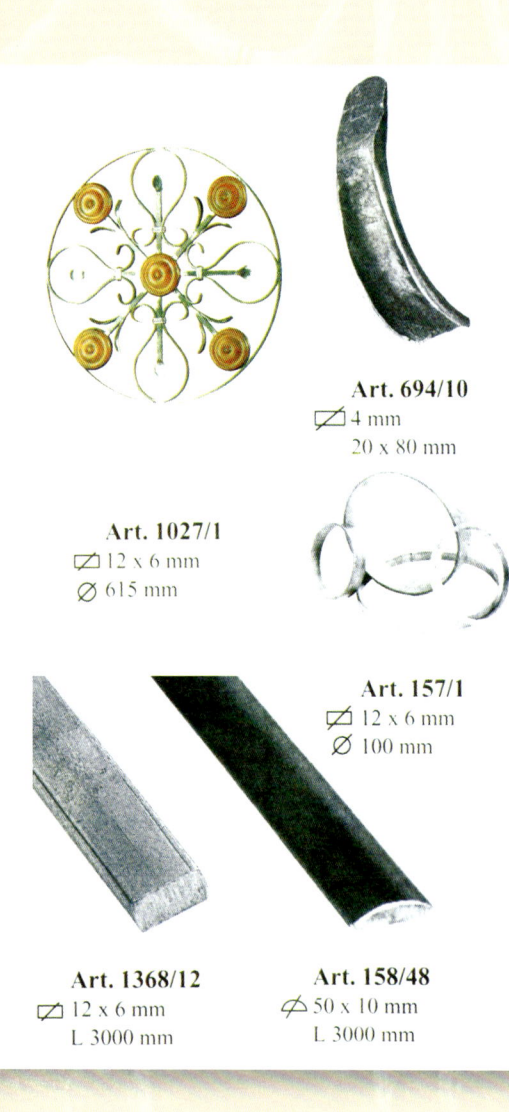

Art. 694/10
◻ 4 mm
20 x 80 mm

Art. 1027/1
◻ 12 x 6 mm
⌀ 615 mm

Art. 157/1
◻ 12 x 6 mm
⌀ 100 mm

Art. 1368/12
◻ 12 x 6 mm
L 3000 mm

Art. 158/48
⌀ 50 x 10 mm
L 3000 mm

Produzione: ind.i.a. SPA

220

Gratings

Art. 118/A/6
◇ 30 x 8 mm
L 3000 mm

Art. 1061/1
⌀ 12 mm
205 x 1000 mm

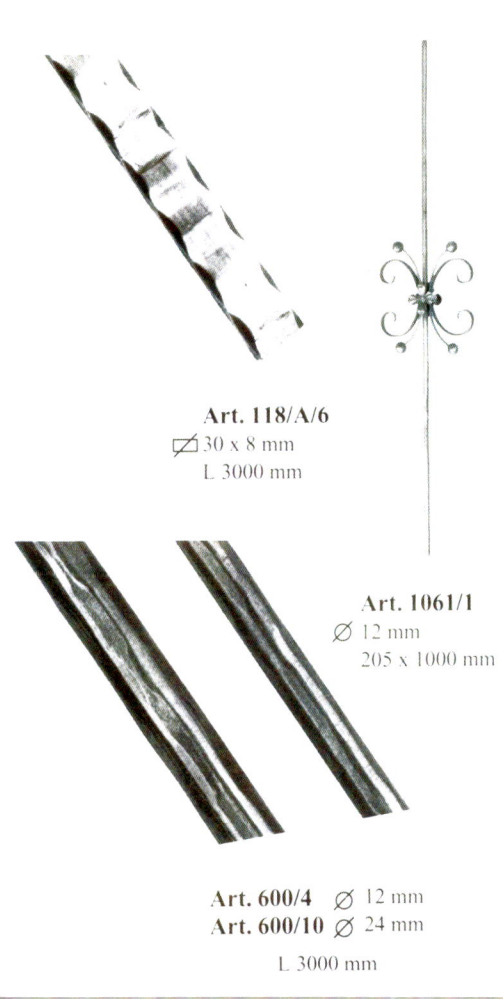

Art. 600/4 ⌀ 12 mm
Art. 600/10 ⌀ 24 mm
L 3000 mm

Produzione: ind.i.a. SPA

221

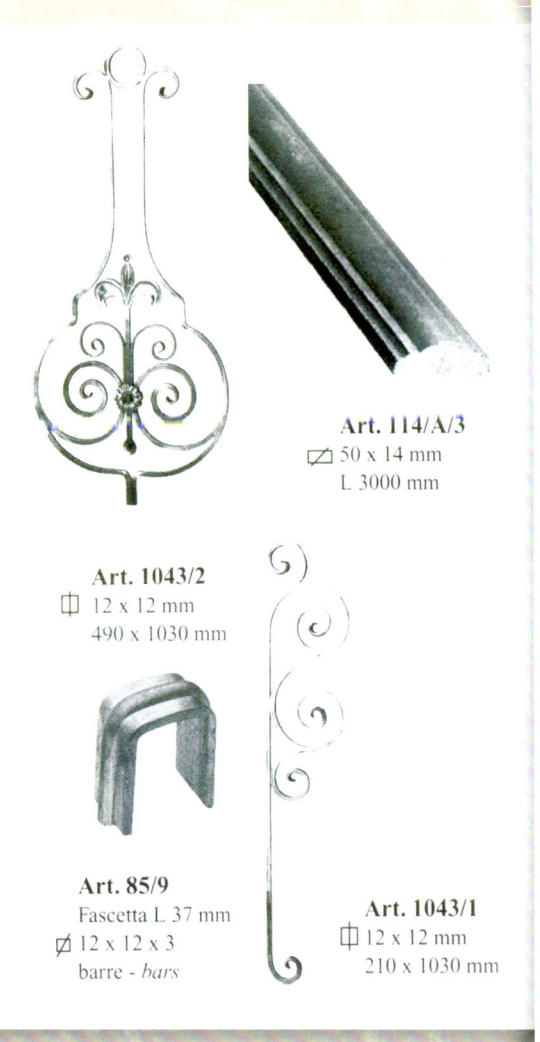

Gratings

Art. 114/A/3
50 x 14 mm
L 3000 mm

Art. 1043/2
12 x 12 mm
490 x 1030 mm

Art. 85/9
Fascetta L 37 mm
12 x 12 x 3
barre - bars

Art. 1043/1
12 x 12 mm
210 x 1030 mm

Produzione: ind.i.a. SPA

222

Gratings

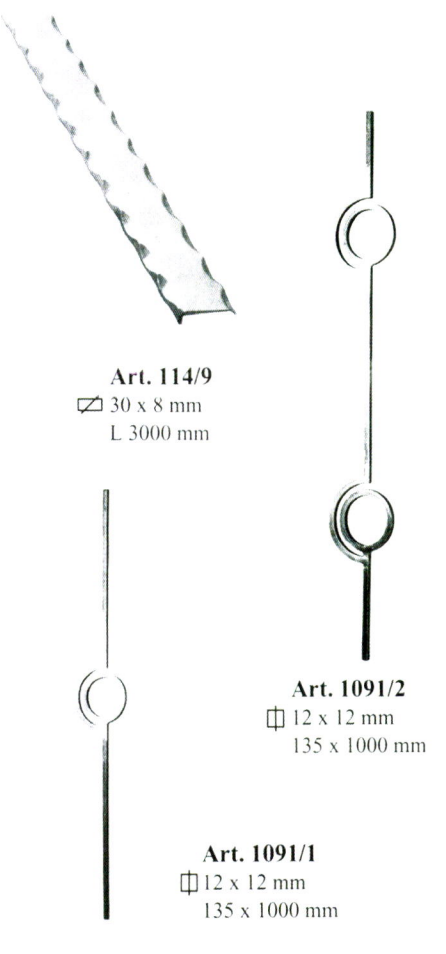

Art. 114/9
◇ 30 x 8 mm
L 3000 mm

Art. 1091/2
□ 12 x 12 mm
135 x 1000 mm

Art. 1091/1
□ 12 x 12 mm
135 x 1000 mm

Produzione: ind.i.a. SPA

Gratings

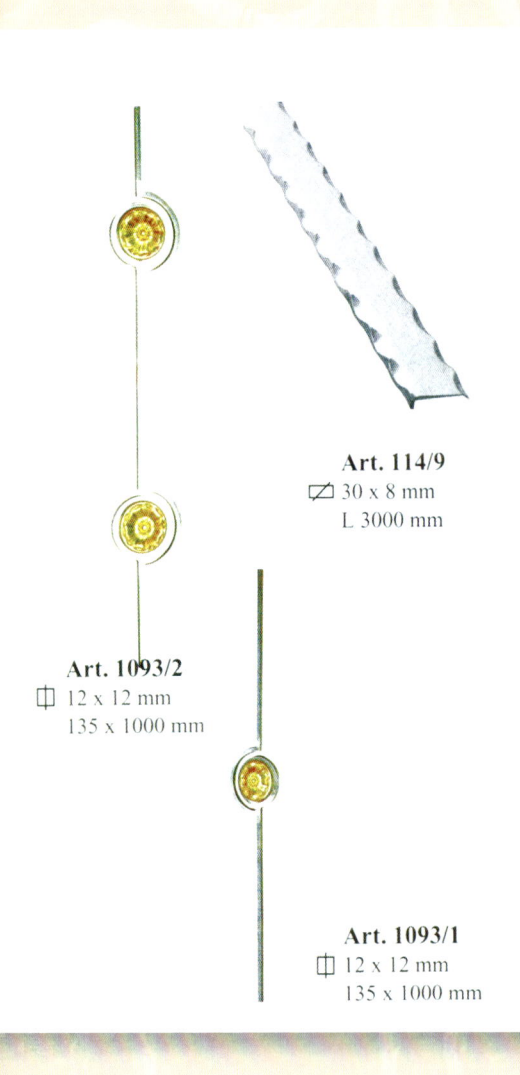

Art. 114/9
⌀ 30 x 8 mm
L 3000 mm

Art. 1093/2
☐ 12 x 12 mm
135 x 1000 mm

Art. 1093/1
☐ 12 x 12 mm
135 x 1000 mm

Produzione: ind.i.a. SPA

224

Gratings

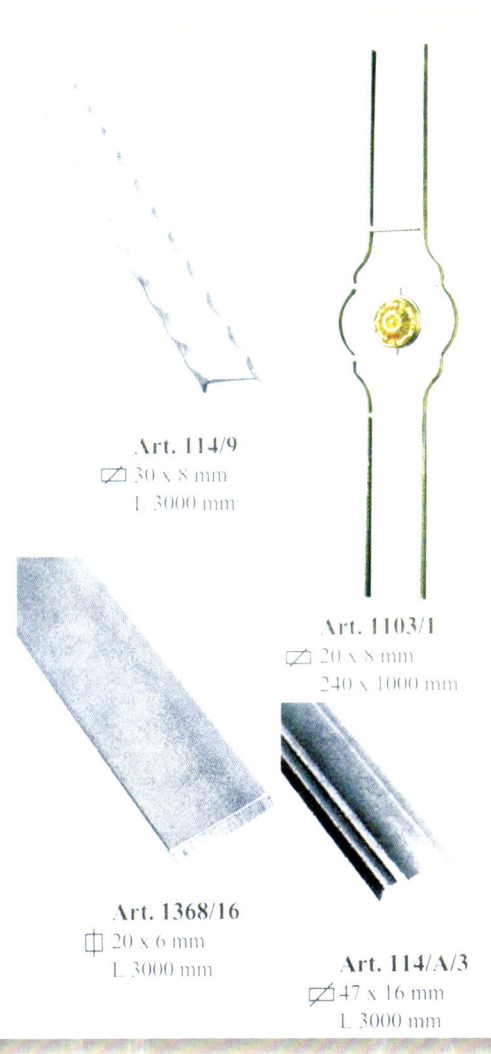

Art. 114/9
◇ 30 x 8 mm
L. 3000 mm

Art. 1103/1
◇ 20 x 8 mm
240 x 1000 mm

Art. 1368/16
□ 20 x 6 mm
L. 3000 mm

Art. 114/A/3
◇ 47 x 16 mm
L. 3000 mm

Produzione: ind.i.a. SPA

225

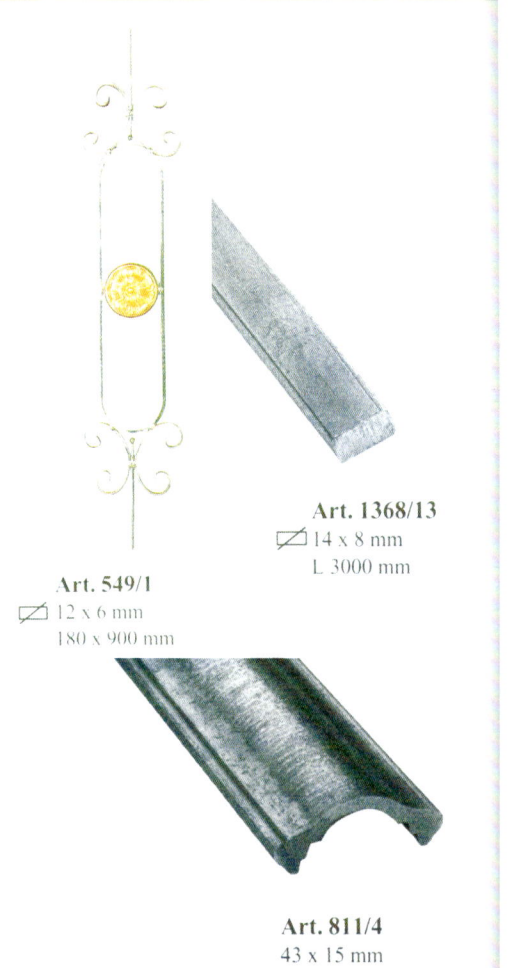

Gratings

Art. 549/1
12 x 6 mm
180 x 900 mm

Art. 1368/13
14 x 8 mm
L 3000 mm

Art. 811/4
43 x 15 mm
L 3000 mm

Produzione: ind.i.a. SPA

Gratings

Art. 587/42
12 x 12 mm
H 1000 mm

Art. 570/1
12 x 12 mm
140 x 900 mm

Art. 114/A/3
50 x 14 mm
L 3000 mm

Art. 634/4
12 x 12 mm
160 x 225 mm

Produzione: ind.i.a. SPA

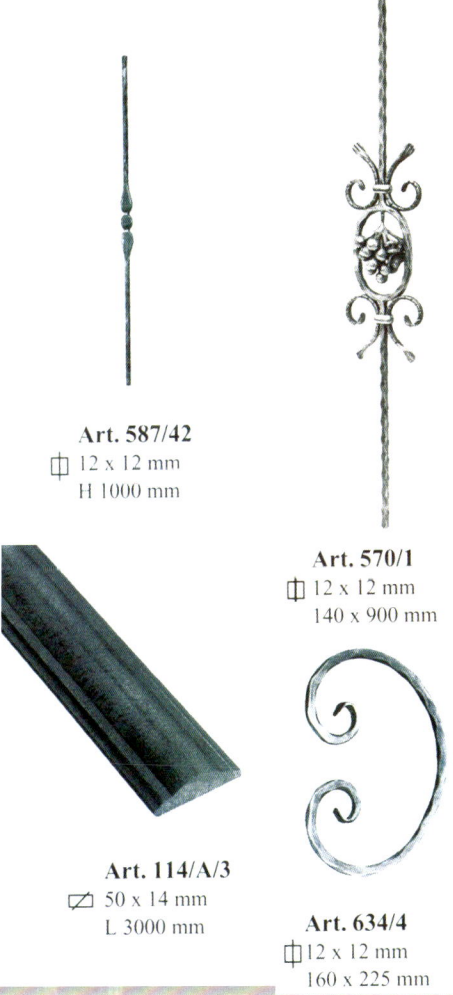

Gratings

Art. 114/9
30 x 8 mm
L 3000 mm

Art. 1105/1
12 x 12 mm
210 x 1000 mm

Art. 1368/4
12 mm
L 3000 mm

Produzione: ind.i.a. SPA

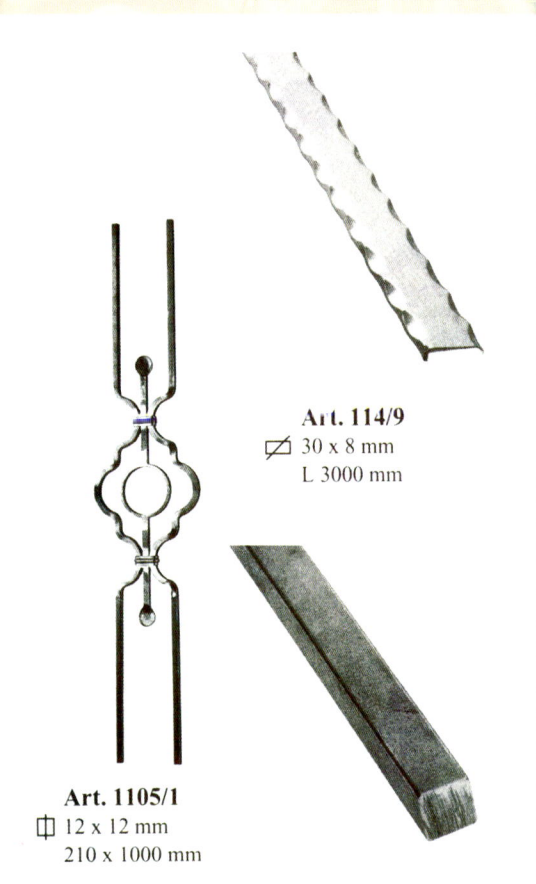

228

Gratings

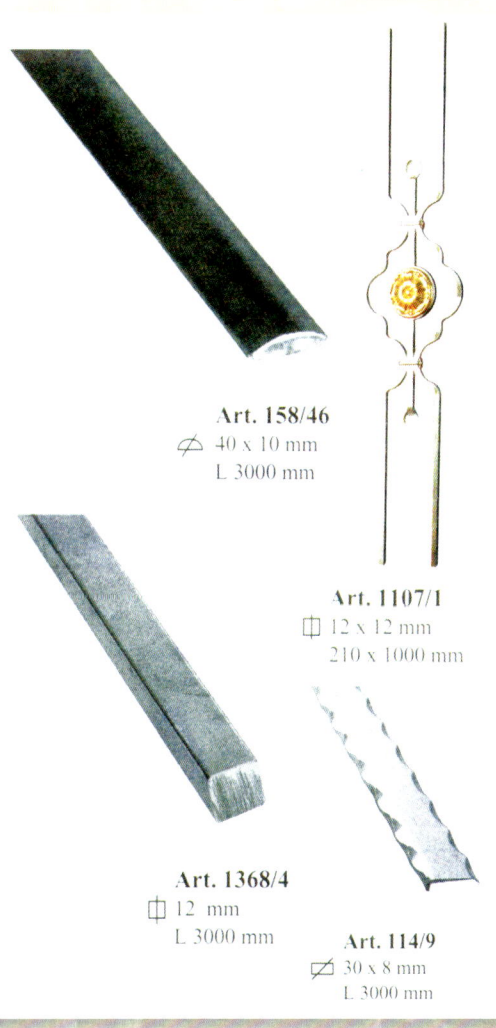

Art. 158/46
⌀ 40 x 10 mm
L 3000 mm

Art. 1107/1
□ 12 x 12 mm
210 x 1000 mm

Art. 1368/4
□ 12 mm
L 3000 mm

Art. 114/9
⌀ 30 x 8 mm
L 3000 mm

Produzione: ind.i.a. SPA

229

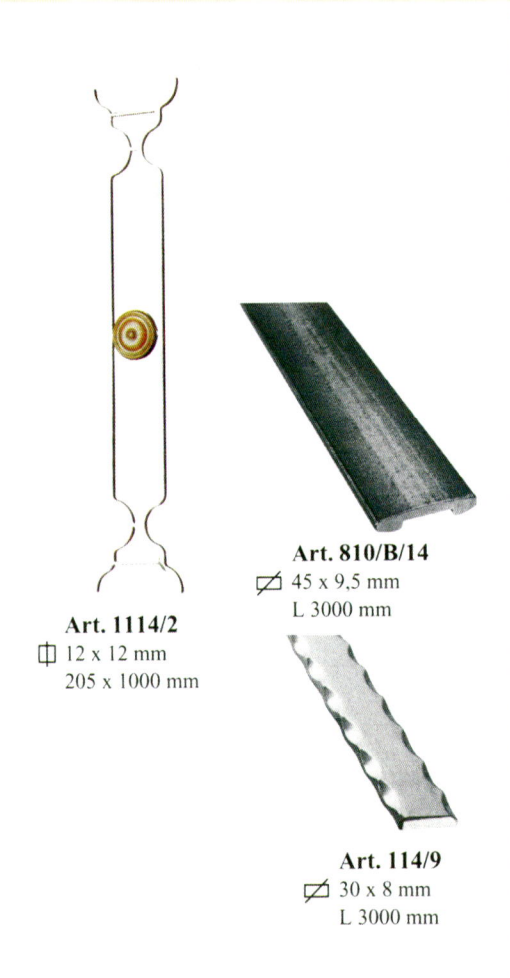

Gratings

Art. 1114/2
12 x 12 mm
205 x 1000 mm

Art. 810/B/14
45 x 9,5 mm
L 3000 mm

Art. 114/9
30 x 8 mm
L 3000 mm

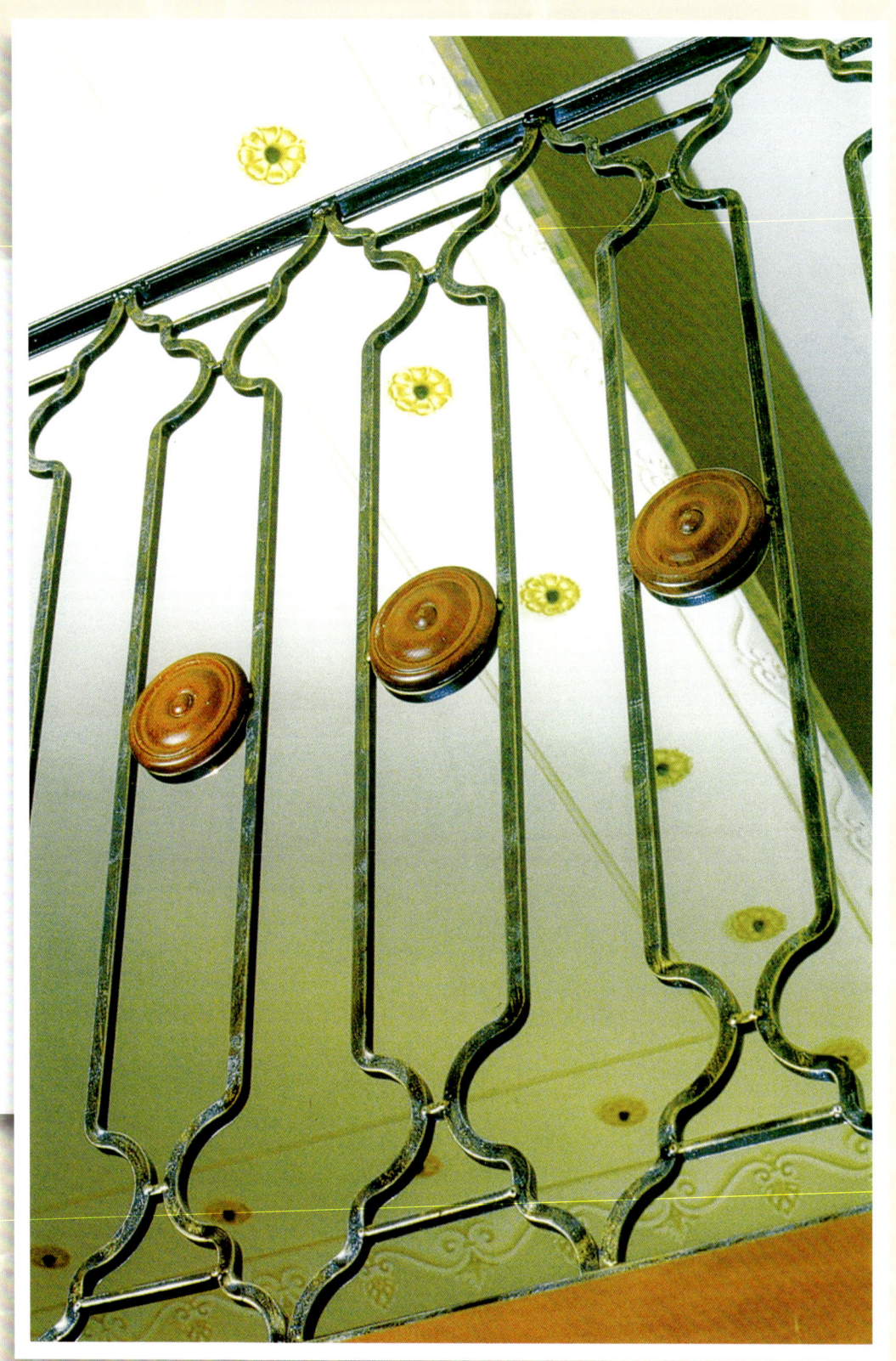

Produzione: ind.i.a. SPA

Gratings

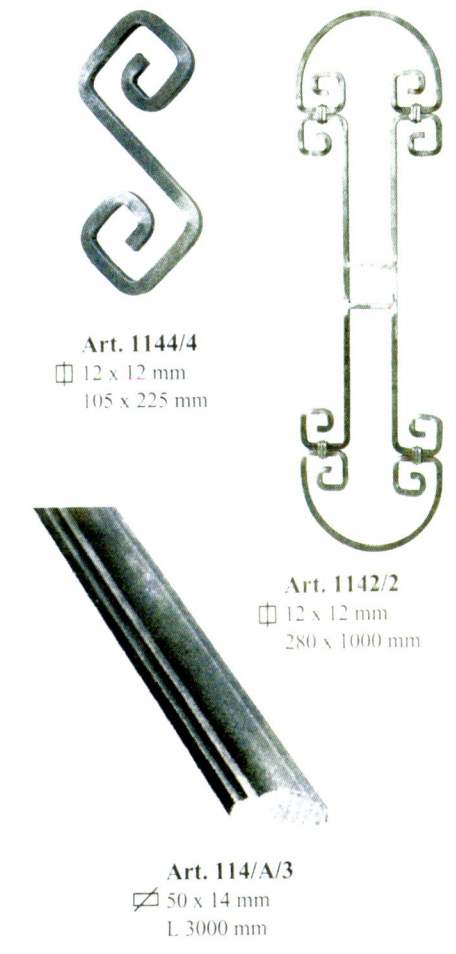

Art. 1144/4
12 x 12 mm
105 x 225 mm

Art. 1142/2
12 x 12 mm
280 x 1000 mm

Art. 114/A/3
50 x 14 mm
L 3000 mm

Produzione: ind.i.a. SPA

Gratings

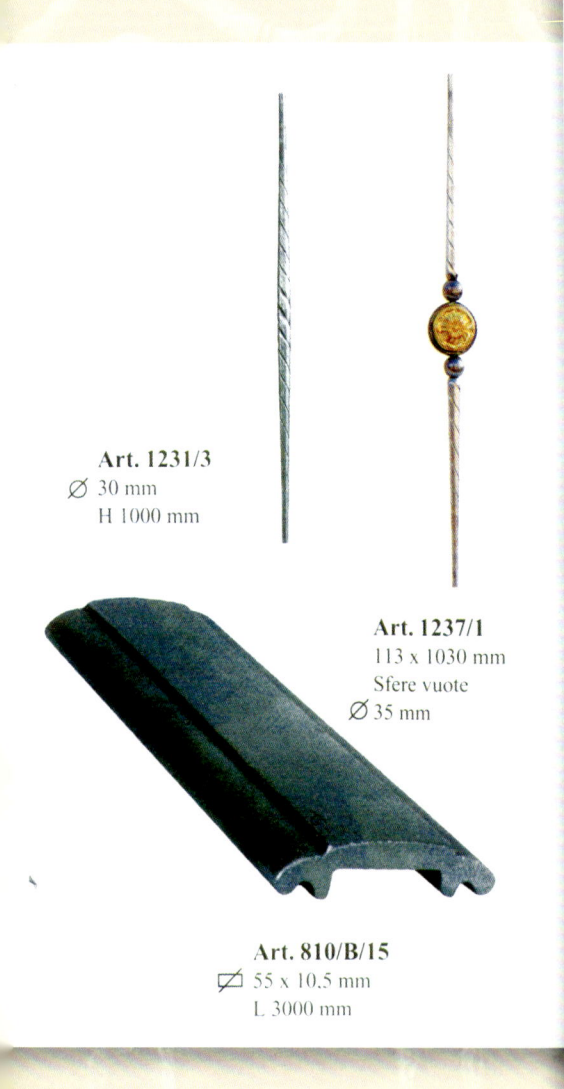

Art. 1231/3
⌀ 30 mm
H 1000 mm

Art. 1237/1
113 x 1030 mm
Sfere vuote
⌀ 35 mm

Art. 810/B/15
◻ 55 x 10.5 mm
L 3000 mm

Produzione: ind.i.a. SPA

Furniture

Products: Ind.i.aSPA

Furniture

Tables, Beds, Radiator Shutters and Chest

In recent years, the blacksmith products have experienced a revival, as it's not so difficult to find some young furniture designers who would entrust the blacksmith artists for the execution of their artworks.

The principal trend of this industry is to recover the styles belonging to the past and to propose again the style which is "renewed and corrected" from the point of view of construction techniques. Regarding the forging of tables, they are usually made from a marble or crystal tabletop and a wrought iron table base. These present a style with sinuous plank with extreme curls in the exterior and a turn-back in the interior in order to keep the balance of the whole structure. They are produced differently according to tabletop shape of round or triangle.

Some small tables of wrought iron reuse the shapes of French style in 19th century. They are made from an iron tabletop in the shape of cylinder. The top will be barbed with three lances which are fixed in the middle by an iron clamp.

Furniture

Another application of wrought iron to the furniture is for the beds and headboards. The usage of metal beds spreads in a world where only few are looking forward to having the mental beds. In fact, in 17th century in the French palace, the beds for the young dauphins and their rulers were made from metal in order to toughen their futures which were ruled by a rigorous military life from their childhood. The beds, which are forged in 1803 by the Paris blacksmith Desouches, held remarkable historical importance. They came from Napoleone Bonapate, who used this kind of beds during his military campaign. These foldable, strong and robust beds were made for the aim of being portable during the journeys between battlefields.

From this moment, the bed becomes not only an object with great practicality but also a workpiece that shows the inspiration and art. The productions of headboards are still quite common now. They are sometimes decorated heavily and sometimes quite simple and linear. Tracing back to the beginning of 20th century, the so-called radiator shutters are used mainly to hide the less refined radiators with a cover which adopts the same style as the whole room. Usually, it is made from a mixture of woods and iron in order to facilitate the diffusion of heat in the surroundings.

It is acclaimed many times that the iron is quite suitable for different furniture thanks to its practical and less decorative features. In the whole period from late Middle Ages to Liberty style, thanks to wrought iron, all sorts of grill gate, grating, utensil, lock become an element of furniture with undeniable artistic value.

Now in the wake of different blacksmith arts of past epoch, people create objects for the aim of ornaments. We can take cloth hangers as an example. They are usually placed in a house with modern furniture to give a sense of originality to the entire style. They are fixed directly on the wall and leave outside only some knobs to hang up the clothes. Or they are made up from simple frames and decorated with flower motifs with twisted arms placed in vertical.

Furniture

They represent furniture with tastes and also accessories with great practicality.

Another element from ancient tastes but not so rare should be found on the gates of villas or modern buildings. It is called "little woodpecker" or knocker for the external gates.

Of course it makes more sense in a time when there was no doorphone and the only way to contact the owner of house was to knock the door. In the historical centers of different cities, these rings are massively made from wrought iron for decoration. The little woodpeckers have different typologies. The ring is deformed till having an oval shape or the knocker's body looks like a lira.

If we divide ideally the different zones of Italy, we would find that in Toscana and the rest of central Italy the most popular shape of the woodpecker is a ring with zoomorphic or geometrical decorations. Instead in the north of Italy, the hammered shape is typical. With hammer, the zoomorphic motifs become the little woodpeckers. Generally from 16th century, it is quite often to see some knockers shaped of a junction of a hand which held a branch of bay tree ending up with a lion.

Furniture

Countless knockers use simple shapes with sober and curved lines to make the figure of animals of gentle or aggressive looks.

We have already understood how the wrought iron is not only used for the heavy gratings or grills of high value, but also for the small objects. For example, the iron handles for the gates release an ancient smell and meanwhile they are also strong with particular antioxidant treatments.

In fact, the iron handles from the traditional wavy and flower-like motifs on the plate which are fixed on the gate would make the wood gate more special. Or they would embellish the gate with a pommel. Any object, both an architectural element and a furniture, could be decorated and become more precious with curls, spirals, twisted lines and flower figures, which could be installed initially in the structure or designed ad hoc to refine the style of the building or the villa which need be decorated.

Lamps and Chandeliers

The most ancient examples of lamps use a fuel of liquid grease which is put in a

Furniture

Produzione: ind.i.a. SPA

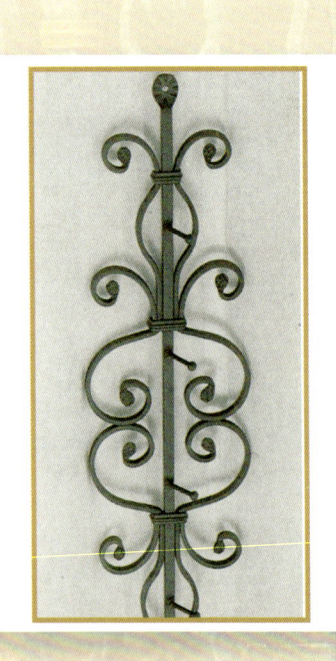

Furniture

container. The fuses or so-called wicks are soaked in the container. The liquid which is absorbed for the capillarity will burn in the extremity of the wicks.

Through centuries, the lighting styles experience different evolutions. They are made from different materials like terracotta and iron. The first iron lamps belong to the 14th century and they are portable or fixed. The portable ones have a thin iron barrel with a ring on the top and an expanded base. So they become an oil tank with one or more burners.

Between 15th and 16th century, the lamps take diverse shapes of classic inspirations, while between 17th and 18th century, the droplights become decorated by gold and silver or become carved to decorate the interior of the buildings and churches.

More of the introductions of the gas lamp, a radical innovation of lights is the birth of electrical lamps. They demonstrate the spirit of the modern times which combines both the practicality and efficiency. The wrought iron is limited to be used for the decorated lamp base which supports the lightshade. Or the iron is used to particular types of lamps. In fact, some lamps are

Furniture

designed in an special way and so they can be placed on the tables or on the desks. In this case the entire lamp, including the lampshade, is made from wrought iron.

In comparison with lamps, the chandeliers are symbolized with the traits as being suspended and applied to a convenient height in order to illuminate the entire surroundings as well as to decorate the environment. Although people give the name of chandelier to some kind of lamps already present in Middle Age, the usage of this kind of artificial illumination devices becomes popular with the adoption of wax candles especially in the private houses.

The first chandeliers are made for one or more candles, which are normally placed in a circle, supported by arms and hang from the high. And therefore, they place the lights in the center of house. The chandeliers vary from the centers and the arms according to diverse period and locations.

In the Middle Age, the chandeliers are made in the shape of a circle or a crown in addition to the shape of horizontal cross. The Gothic style prefers more simple lines, structures with rigid barrels and more

Furniture

arms which would be separated in one or more orders.

The favorite material for chandeliers in this moment is indeed the iron. And this inclination continues till the Renaissance during which the ornamental materials for the chandeliers has enriched by glass, china or hard stones. So as the lamps, also the chandeliers experience great evolution with the introduction of electrical ones. The electrical chandeliers keep the same shape as the classic ones, but also add the appropriate modifications according to the new technologies. The classical iron chandeliers should be rectangular with diverse candles placed on the longer side. Or they should be round, for example with three candles placed in three different points of the circumference, and raise up according to their characters to the end of three curved vertical arms.

Reassuming the decoration styles of 17th century, today people also forge the chandeliers with more arms which were designed with a flower in the center. From above the arms look twisted like climbing plants. From this shape which could be defined as classic style, now the chandeliers have passed to a decisively more modern style. More vertical arms are

Furniture

applied in accordance with the central axis. And from the axis, the arms twisted as hooks.

Lanterns and Candle Holders

Another application of wrought iron, which brings us a lot of masterpiece creations, is for the products of lanterns and corridor lights.

The time when people focus on this kind of production is 16th century, when the lanterns, together with the grill gates at the entrance of the buildings, represent the elements of greatest impact.

Due to the iron's quality of a material resistant to all the atmospheric factors, the iron is preferred, for example than the woods, to be applied for the manufacture of lightings in the exterior of the halls and courtyards of the buildings and villas.

Moreover, although the lanterns have a main function of practicality, they also show the style of the entire building. In this case, the lanterns placed in a liberty-styled lobby follow the style of the flower figures of grill gates, in order to maintain the syntony and harmony. But this concept of harmonizing the same style with the grill gates is limited only for the arms of suspension, in order not to obstacle the

Furniture

main function which is to illuminate.

Some examples of the lanterns belonging to 15th century are present in Siena, where the tendency of the forging shapes is geometrical and the figures of little dragons both on the base, and on the top of pillars give life to the lightshade of the flames. Other examples are located instead in Turin.

In Turin, the style is simpler and totally lack of decorations.

The lanterns can be placed not only at the entrance of the corridors and in the lobbies, but also in the staircase of the buildings.

Naturally, in this case the lanterns contain more dimensions to adapt themselves to a smaller space. They are also decorated in a more complicated way to reduce the illuminating surface.

When they are placed in the lobbies of the buildings, sometimes lanterns can be fixed on the ceiling or on the interior and the exterior facade of the buildings.

In some time, the lanterns placed on the exterior facade of the buildings are considered as unique illuminating source, together with lamps of the aedicules and the movable lanterns.

Furniture

One of the greatest forgers of the lanterns was Niccolò Grosso, called Caparra, who is the creator of many remarkable products of lanterns in the Renaissance buildings in Florence. It is Caparra who brought the art of iron lanterns to the highest level during his stay in the courts of Medici. He makes all his creatures in miniature with lots of chapiters, mullioned windows, columns and archways, which form a sort of tiny time.

The lanterns are designed in this way also for the aim of decorating the too simple Renaissance facade of Florence buildings.

Another great forger of the lanterns is Alessandro Mazzucotelli, who was already introduced before. We know that he is a great forger of grills, gratings and gates of excellent beauty in the Liberty style in famous buildings of Lombardi. Mazzucotelli is the creator of the most special lanterns which were decorated with zoomorphic figures. Like butterflies, they are refined in a detailed way and are placed on the lanterns.

Andirons and Cooking Utensils

Furniture

There are numerous objects of wrought iron with a specifically practical function in the surroundings. In diverse times these objects play a rather important role of furniture. The utensils, from andirons, for example, or those for cooking, have an ancient history and till now people still follow it.

The andirons are aflame on the fireplace which serve to support the woods and the fuel. And usually they are present in a couple. The very first andirons are made from stones and function in a practical way to support the different containers in addition to the woods. From the beginning they are made from metals which make them more resistant and stronger to hold the largest weight. There is a metal horizontal beam placed on some 60 cm supporting items and folded up at both ends. Later the lanterns in the noble houses transform according to the surroundings full of ornaments. In the Middle Age in coincidence with the developments of the domestic chimneys which sometimes have a monumental structure, iron andirons of notable ornaments are highly demanded. Some elements are continuously used in all the ages, like the tripod front base and beam which supported the skewers. The Gothic

Furniture

style enriches the design of andirons. And the figures of branches, leaves and snakes prevail.

During the Renaissance, the andirons start to show in the noble halls. There are full of golden decorative figures created by famous sculptures of the age.

Till now the andirons still maintain duplicate functions of both practicality and decoration. They are usually installed in the rural houses with chimneys.

Although the evidences of the iron cooking utensils which belong to other ages are really rare, their discoveries still hold a significant value, because they reveal the eating habit and testify the evolution degree of different population, even the ancient ones.

Modern cookers which are made in a traditional way, for example fixed on the wall, have the characteristics named panoply. It is made from two metal belts fixed on the wall to hold two or more small hooks which are used to hang the various cookers.

Furniture

The panoply can become an ornamental object that displays the decorations or flower figure forged in double-ends.

Keys, Locks and Padlocks

The wrought iron makes possible the creation of any objects and in addition also realizes the decorative purpose, besides the fact that it has a practical function.

Like the keys, they are forged according to the stylistic standards of the time in different ages.

Some examples of Middle Age keys reveal the simplicity and linearity of the art of 13th century. They are mostly shaped as the thin tubes or flat and rectangular plugs. The keys are also equipped with different intaglios.

Different from the ancient keys, the rings are more maneuverable with the round or rhomboidal shape. Sometimes it is open on the top or has some flat or enlarged angles. Close to the late Gothic period, the key ring is processed with thin iron slats and becomes more precious for the elegant annulus and other typical decorative figures. During the Renaissance, the rings are also symbolized with figure of branches, the same style as the matching locks.

The decorations pierced on the handles are quite precious. The decorative figures are enriched by the graver or etching.

Without any doubt, the apogee of the artistic production of keys undergoes in the Baroque Age, as all the other iron products. The beauty of the objects prevails universally on the basis of practicality. In fact the decoration of keys is to forge them on both faces with a moving ring or to add some other materials such as gold or silver to make the keys and locks more expensive. In this case we can see the symbolic keys of the cities where the precious decorations are also spread to other objects.

For the practical use, the locks and keys are an undividable unit. From the ancient time, a lot of cares are dedicated to them. The lock is a fundamental element for the gates. It always exists from the time it was made from woods and becomes more precisely from the time it was used in Egypt.

The components of the locks are: bolt and door fixture, whose functions are different in the course of centuries. In history the lock has three diverse applications according to their end user. There are locks for gates, locks for trunks and padlocks.

The Gothic locks are equipped with an elementary mechanism until in 15th century spring latch and latch lever appear. Some samples of that period which are kept till now show some embossed decorations of vegetal motifs on the lock plate which should cover the mechanism.

A turning point in the area of locks happens in the Renaissance when people start to adopt the closure system smartly and to work with extreme precision. There is a difference in the past. The keys could be operated easily into the close locks.

Naturally with the transform of the mechanism, the way to fix the locks on the doors changes as well.

Furniture

On the contrary as designed in the Gothic period when the mechanism should be covered under a plate, in the Renaissance, it is placed in a visible place on the internal side of the gate. So a problem is proposed: how to make it look nice.

In the beginning, the decoration is limited to the massive plate with nails notched on the edge and decorated with flowers to fix on the door.

In a second time also the mechanism itself is decorated with vegetal or zoomorphic motifs and sometimes also absurd figures which are popular during that time. The locks of Baroque Age have bigger plates and decorated elaborately. At the end of 18th century, the golden period of the lock manufacture terminates, although in the first half of 19th century there are some refined samples.

Starting from the Gothic Age, also the padlocks experience various transformations as the locks.

From the beginning the padlocks are mainly used practically and never for the decorative purpose. It has a linear shape, like heart, cylinder and sphere.

Furniture

More decorations are applied when the padlocks assume importance as artworks in the Renaissance. In the 17th and 18th century, there are combination padlocks or double key padlocks, which need two different keys.

The keys to open a padlock are completely similar with the keys to any locks. But sometime it could be various. They shape like an eye bolt with a long thread which arrives to the ring. These keys are generally shaped of rings.

To open the door with this kind of keys it is necessary to screw the keys, while to close the door, people need unscrew the keys. In the 18th century and in the beginning of 19th century, the popular padlocks have invisible keyholes and only the owners know what to do to find the holes.

Mazzucotelli

Some works of blacksmiths master Alessandro Mazzucotelli. Above, grill gate and railing of Villa Mazzotti, Brescia 1911. Middle, the staircase in the Castiglioni Palace, in C.so Venezia in Milan. The palace was built in 1903 by Fratelli Galimberti and designed by well-known Arc. Sommaruga.

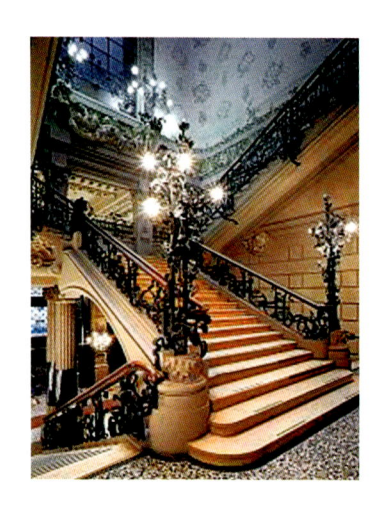

Below are details of the works of Mazzucotelli

Mazzucotelli

The beginning of 20th century is a period that witnessed works by the greatest blacksmith master of all the ages and also the last master who has left important blacksmith artworks—Alessandro Mazzucotelli. He was born in Lodi in 1865 and worked in all the cities of Lombardia. Especially in Monza and Milan, there are many remarkable products from his workshop. He is the founder of workshop Bicocca, near Milan. The last iron artisans and creators, together with their master, came from this workshop. They created the grill gates of Columbus Clinic of Milan, or the lamps of typical liberty style which are decorated with animals or flowers, and lanterns which are decorated with butterflies of natural size. His work is from the smallest ornamental objects to the large grill gates of both public and private buildings.

In the works of Marzzucotelli, the nature occupies the leading role, together with motifs of animals and plants (flowers, leaves, dragonflies, butterflies, roosters and also goats and monkeys), which have filled all his creations.

Building in Via Malpighi, Milan 1902
The balconies convey the justice to the artistic capacity of the most important Italian blacksmiths Master: Alessandro Muzzucotelli (1865-1938)

Mazzucotelli

Art. 690/3
∅ 12 mm
70 x 112 x 5 m
70 x 112 x 5 mm

Art. 690/2
∅ 12 mm
160 x 80 x 5 mm

Most of the grill gates in Milan and in Monza in this period, come from his workshop. He is well known also for the combination of iron and glass. Mazzucotelli used to combine them to maximize the transparency. An example of grill gate of this artist is the gate of Casa Campanini in Milan. It shows a double structure, which is completely innovative in comparison with all the precedent works. In fact it is a grill gate with the function of "mobile screen" in the daytime, as well as with the defensive function in the night.

Mazzucotelli

Art. 662/5
◇ 16 x 6 mm
150 x 250 mm

Art. 662/3
∅ 12 mm
65 x 130 mm

Art. 662/1
◇ 16 x 8 mm
105 x 220 mm

Art. 662/6
◇ 16 x 6 mm
150 x 250 mm

Therefore with new technologies Mazzucotelli succeeded to make different functions of grill gates live together. In fact in the gate of Casa Campanini, the transit from "mobile screen" to the real gate works by a system called "little swallower". With this system, the grill gate moves vertically until it is swallowed by the flooring.

Mazzucotelli and his students were the last important representatives of blacksmith art of the 20th century, not only for the exhaustion of art, but also for the passing-away of the great iron artist who was both the executive and the designer of this era.

ARTPOWER

Acknowledgements
We would like to thank all the designers and companies who made significant contributions to the compilation of this book. Without them, this project would not have been possible. We would also like to thank many others whose names did not appear on the credits, but made specific input and support for the project from beginning to end.

Future Editions
If you would like to contribute to the next edition of Artpower, please email us your details to: artpower@artpower.com.cn